The Kitchen
Companion

Photography
Cut-out photographs: Paul Turner and Sue Pressley,
    Stonecastle Graphics Ltd, Marden, Kent
Recipe photographs: Colour Library Books

Design
Paul Turner and Sue Pressley, Stonecastle Graphics Ltd

Editorial
Compiled and edited: Wendy Hobson

Typesetting
DSP, Maidstone, Kent

Jacket
Photography: Stonecastle Graphics Ltd

Production
Ruth Arthur
Sally Connolly
Andrew Whitelaw

Director of production
Gerald Hughes

CLB 3191
© 1992 Colour Library Books Ltd, Godalming, Surrey.
All rights reserved.
Colour Separation by Scantrans PTE Ltd, Singapore.
Printed and bound by Imprimerie Pollina S.A., France. n° 15109
ISBN 0 86283 979 3

The Kitchen Companion

Your Seasonal Guide to Delicious Recipes

Compiled and edited by Wendy Hobson

CLB

Colour Library Books

Making the Most of the Seasons

EVERY SEASON and every month of the year has its own special associations: from the rich and warming soups which ward off the cold of a January day to the luscious soft fruits of summer, the crisp russet apples of autumn, and all the traditional delights of the Christmas season.

The Kitchen Companion contains a seasonal selection of recipes, hints and tips to help you make the best of foods in season and create tasty dishes all the year round. Of course, you do not have to restrict yourself to making the dishes just at one particular time of the year, for you are sure to find favourites you will want to cook again and again.

Many foods are now available in the supermarket throughout the year, and are often of excellent quality, even when out of season. But they can be more expensive so watch out for both price and quality. It is often the best idea to use foods when they are in season, particularly fruits and vegetables. Not only are they cheapest at that time, the flavour will be at its best. You may be able to buy lovely-looking Brussels sprouts in March, but the taste could be bitter and will not compare with the sweet, nutty sprouts you can buy at Christmas. Tomatoes are available all the year round, but you will find the tastiest, juiciest ones are those which have ripened under a summer sun. And with every month offering you a different selection of produce, there is always something to look forward to.

Try to use fresh produce where possible. It will not only taste the best, but is also the best for you, as it will contain its full complement of vitamins and minerals. Avoid buying foods which look faded or tired; they are past their best.

If you are short of time to prepare fresh foods or want to use produce out of season, look for canned or frozen varieties, many of which offer excellent value and quality. Keep a basic store cupboard so that you can always put together something interesting at short notice.

Many of the recipes in this book are simple and quick to prepare, so they are ideal for the busy household where you need a tasty and nutritious meal without complicated preparation or long cooking times.

All the recipes are simply presented so you can see at a glance what you need and how to prepare it. There are many suggestions for variations to recipes, and you can always experiment to make your own versions of the dishes. If you do not have a particular ingredient, just look through the recipe and see whether you can leave it out, or substitute something else you have in the cupboard. Never be afraid to try out new ideas of your own, especially using foods which you have grown yourself, which are in season or readily available.

You will not need any special kitchen equipment. Of course, if you have a food processor, blender or mixer, do use them to speed up slicing, chopping, blending or any other preparation.

Cooking Tips

THESE HANDY tips will help you to make the best of your *Kitchen Companion*.

1 Store foods carefully to maintain their freshness. Always remove plastic wrappings as they will cause foods to sweat. Store fruits and vegetables on a cool shelf or at the bottom of the refrigerator. Wrap cheese or cooked meats in foil and store in the refrigerator, removing cheese 1 hour before serving to allow it to ripen. Place raw meats on a plate, cover well and make sure they do not come into contact with other foods in the refrigerator.

2 Look out for sell-by dates when you are shopping and use up fresh foods by the date indicated.

3 Always wash fresh produce before preparation.

4 Eggs are size 2. If you do not have large eggs, simply add a little more or less liquid to the mixture to obtain the correct consistency.

5 Follow one set of measurements only, do not mix metric and Imperial.

6 Spoon measurements are level. It is best to use a set of measuring spoons as they are accurate and easy to use. Spoons meant for serving food vary in size according to the design.

7 Adjust seasoning and strongly-flavoured ingredients, such as onions and garlic, to suit your own taste. If you are not keen on a particularly strong spice or flavouring, leave it out or substitute something else.

8 Use fresh herbs where possible as they will give you the best flavour and texture. There are only a few exceptions, such as oregano, the flavour of which develops when it is properly dried. If you do substitute dried for fresh herbs, use only half the amount specified but do not use dried herbs for garnish or adding at the end of a recipe or they will taste raw.

9 Always use freshly ground black pepper for seasoning. If you do not use salt in your cooking, you may like to add a few additional herbs.

10 For convenience, the recipes list 'butter', but you can substitute your usual margarine if you prefer.

11 If you do not have a particular cooking pot indicated in the recipe, look at the photograph and select the most suitable item you have.

12 Cooking times are given in °C, °F and gas marks. Because ovens vary, these are approximate and may need to be adjusted to suit your oven. Fan ovens, for example, will need lower temperatures and the food will take less time to cook. You know your own oven best so adjust times and temperatures to suit, if necessary.

13 All the recipes serve 4 unless otherwise indicated.

Kitchen Store Cupboard

A WELL-STOCKED store cupboard means you can always prepare a simple but tasty meal at those times when you need to put together something from nothing! Use these suggestions to give you more ideas.

Bottles and jars: honey, jam, oil, syrup.
Cans: different kinds of beans, corned beef, fruits in natural juice, pulses, salmon, tuna.
Dry goods: baking powder, bicarbonate of soda, cocoa powder, custard powder, flour, oatmeal, pasta, rice, sponge fingers or biscuits, stock cubes, sugar.
Frozen goods: bread, cream, filo pastry, fish fillets, prawns, puff pastry.
Fruits and nuts: almonds, ground almonds, dried fruits, walnuts.

Herbs and spices: cayenne pepper, cinnamon, curry powder, nutmeg, oregano, mixed herbs, parsley, pepper, salt.
Miscellaneous: butter, eggs, chocolate, jelly, long-life milk.
Sauces: tomato purée, Worcester sauce.
Vegetables: carrots, onions, potatoes.

Bean Salad: Drain, rinse and mix a selection of canned beans. Dress with French dressing (see page iv) and sprinkle with fresh herbs.

Fish Goujons: Coat strips of fish fillet in egg and flour and fry in butter or oil. Serve with a white sauce (see page iv) flavoured with chopped fresh or dried parsley, potatoes and peas.

Prawn Parcels: Make a thick white sauce (see page iv) using half milk and half chicken stock and stir in some prawns. Use to fill little parcels made of layers of filo pastry brushed with oil and twisted together at the top. Brush with oil and bake in a preheated oven at 200°C/400°F/gas mark 6 for 10 minutes.

Corned Beef Fritters: Coat cubes of corned beef in a thick batter (see page iv) and fry until golden.

Tuna Flan: Line a flan ring with shortcrust pastry (see page iv), spread with drained tuna and season with salt, pepper and cayenne pepper. Beat 2 eggs with 150 ml/^{1}/$_4$ pt cream or milk, pour over the tuna and bake in a preheated oven at 200°C/400°F/gas mark 6 for 30 minutes.

Pasta Bowl: Mix cooked pasta with a selection of beans, chopped onion, prawns, or chopped corned beef. Mix with mayonnaise (see page iv) flavoured with tomato purée or curry powder.

Tasty Trifle: Layer sponge fingers or cake and drained tinned fruit in a bowl and use the juice to make a jelly. Spoon the jelly over the fruit and leave to set. Top with custard and decorate with grated chocolate.

Chocolate Cake: Beat together 150 ml/^{1}/$_4$ pt milk, 150 ml/^{1}/$_4$ pt corn oil, 2 eggs, 2 tbsp syrup, 200 g/7 oz plain flour, 150 g/5 oz caster sugar, 2 tbsp cocoa powder, 1 tsp bicarbonate of soda, 1 tsp baking powder. Bake in 2 greased and lined 18 cm/7 in cake tins in a preheated oven at 160°C/325°F/gas mark 3 for 35 minutes. Sandwich together with whipped cream.

Basic Recipes

Stock

1 chicken carcass, meat bones or fish heads, bones and skin	1 onion
1 carrot
1 stick celery

Place the meat or fish in a saucepan with a selection of vegetables to give the stock flavour. Just cover with cold water, bring slowly to the boil and simmer for 1¹/₂ hours. Strain, then return the stock to the pan and boil to reduce the liquid. Use quickly or freeze.

Batter

100 g/4 oz plain flour
a pinch of salt	1 egg
150 ml/¹/₄ pt milk

Beat all the ingredients together until the batter is smooth. Alter the amount of milk to adjust the consistency of the batter.

White Sauce

25 g/1 oz butter
25 g/1 oz plain flour	300 ml/¹/₂ pt milk

Melt the butter, stir in the flour and cook for 1 minute. Whisk in the milk and bring to the boil, stirring continuously until the sauce thickens. Alter the amount of milk used to thicken or thin the sauce.

French Dressing

8 tbsp oil
4 tbsp wine vinegar
2 tsp French mustard
salt and pepper

Shake all the ingredients together well in a screw-top jar.

Mayonnaise

1 egg
1 egg yolk
¹/₂ tsp salt
¹/₂ tsp mustard powder	2 tbsp lemon juice
1 tbsp white wine vinegar
375 ml/13 fl oz oil

Place all the ingredients except the oil in a blender and mix well. Add one-third of the oil and mix again. With the blender running, gradually pour in the remaining oil until the mayonnaise thickens. Flavour, if liked, with spices, herbs or tomato purée.

Basic Bread

1.5 kg/3 lb strong plain flour
2 tbsp salt	1 tbsp easy-mix dried yeast
25 g/1 oz lard
900 ml/1¹/₂ pts warm water

Mix together the flour, salt, dried yeast and lard in a food processor. With the motor running, gradually pour in the water until the mixture forms a dough. Process until smooth and elastic and no longer sticky. Cover and leave to rise for 2 hours. Knead again, place in greased loaf tins, cover and leave to rise for a further 1 hour before baking at 230°C/450°F/gas mark 8 for 40 minutes.

Shortcrust Pastry

225 g/8 oz plain flour
a pinch of salt
50 g/2 oz butter	50 g/2 oz lard
3 tbsp water

Sift the flour and salt. Rub in the butter and lard until the mixture resembles breadcrumbs. Mix in enough water to make a soft pastry. Do not overwork. Use as directed in the recipe.

Cooking for Children

MOST CHILDREN love cooking, and they can have great fun in a well-supervised kitchen making meals for their friends or for the family. Always remember that safety comes first. Teach children to be careful of sharp knives and graters, hot pans, food, foil, ovens and steam. Always supervise children while they are cooking.

Sausage Casserole

450 g/1 lb sausagemeat
2 tbsp plain flour
salt and pepper
1 cooking apple, peeled,
    cored and sliced

1 onion, sliced
1/2 tsp dried mixed herbs
400 g/14 oz canned
    tomatoes

Divide the sausagemeat into 16 equal balls. Sprinkle the flour with salt and pepper and roll the balls in the flour. Place the apple, onion and sausagement balls in an ovenproof dish. Sprinkle with herbs and pour over the tomatoes. Sprinkle with salt and pepper. Cover and cook in a preheated oven at 180°C/350°F/gas mark 4 for 1 hour. Serve with mashed potatoes and peas.

Baked Cheese Fingers

8 large slices brown bread
25 g/1 oz butter
4 slices cheese

1 egg, beaten
150 ml/1/4 pt milk
salt and pepper

Remove the crusts from the bread and spread each slice with butter. Cover 4 pieces of bread with cheese and top with the remaining bread. Cut each sandwich into 3 fingers. Mix the egg and milk and sprinkle with salt and pepper. Dip the sandwiches in the milk mixture and arrange in a shallow ovenproof dish. Pour over any remaining mixture. Bake in a preheated oven at 180°C/350°F/gas mark 4 for 15 minutes. Serve with salad.

Potato Surprises

4 baking potatoes, scrubbed
25 g/1 oz butter
2 tbsp milk

50 g/2 oz cheese, grated
4 eggs

Cut a cross through the skins of the potatoes and bake in a preheated oven at 200°C/400°F/gas mark 6 for 1 hour until soft. Cool. Scoop the potato into a bowl and mash with the butter, milk and cheese. Half-fill each potato skin with the cheese mixture. Break an egg into each one. Cover with the remaining cheese mixture and brown under the grill.

Hot Ham Crusties

4 bread rolls
75 g/3 oz soft margarine
grated rind of 1/2 orange

1 tsp chopped fresh parsley
100 g/4 oz ham, chopped
salt and pepper

Cut a thin slice off the top of each roll. Carefully pull out the centre and crumble into breadcrumbs. Mix the breadcrumbs with all the other ingredients and spoon back into the rolls. Replace the tops and wrap each one completely in kitchen foil. Place on a baking tray and bake in a preheated oven at 190°C/375°F/gas mark 5 for 20 minutes. Serve hot.

Banoffee Pie

10 ginger biscuits
50 g/2 oz butter
1 large banana
1 packet butterscotch Angel
    Delight
300 ml/1/2 pt milk
1 chocolate flake

Place the ginger biscuits in a bag and crush them with a rolling pin. Melt the butter in a saucepan. Remove from the heat and mix in the biscuit crumbs. Press the mixture into the base of a flan ring and leave to cool and set. Slice the banana and arrange the slices on the biscuit base. Whip up the Angel Delight with the milk according to the instructions on the packet. Pour over the banana and leave to set. Decorate with crumbled flake.

Fairy Cakes

200 g/7 oz soft margarine
100 g/4 oz caster sugar
100 g/4 oz plain flour
1 tsp baking powder
2 eggs
175 g/6 oz icing sugar
24 Smarties

Mix together 100 g/4 oz margarine with the sugar, flour, baking powder and eggs until smooth and soft. Spoon the mixture into paper cases in bun tins and bake in a preheated oven at 180°C/350°F/gas mark 4 for about 15 minutes. Place the remaining margarine in a bowl and sift in the icing sugar. Mix together to form icing. (You can colour this with a few drops of food colouring if you wish.) Spread a little on the top of each cooled cake and top with a Smartie.

January

'January brings the snow,
Makes our feet and fingers glow.'
Anon

CHRISTMAS is over and
the New Year begins with resolutions – will we keep them
this year? – with cold winds and winter snows covering
the first snowdrops. The comfort of the kitchen offers
rich and warming winter soups and stews, mellowed with
a spoonful of sherry or wine. The best meals for these
cold days are filling and satisfying to banish the winter
chills. Days are at their shortest now and evenings are
the times to enjoy the cosiness of home.

JANUARY

1 New Year's Day

2 Resolve to try some different cheeses this year: Danish Mycella, Italian Dolcelatte and French Roquefort are all delicious.

3

4 Seville marmalade oranges are in the shops. Squeeze the juice from 1.5 kg/3 lb oranges and 2 lemons. Tie the pips in muslin. Soak the chopped peel overnight in 4 litres/7 pts water. Add the pips and juice and simmer for 1½ hours until the peel is soft. Discard the pips, stir in 2.75 kg/3 lb sugar and boil for 20 minutes until set.

5 Make a winter vegetable soup with chicken stock and your favourite vegetables, purée for a thick soup, then stir in a spoonful of cream.

6 Twelfth Night

7

Onion Soup

900 g/2 lb onions, sliced
2 tsp sugar
50 g/2 oz margarine
50 g/2 oz plain flour
1.5 litres/3 pts chicken or
    vegetable stock
150 ml/¹/₄ pt dry white wine

1 tsp dried thyme
salt and pepper
12 slices French bread
2 tbsp olive oil
25 g/1 oz Cheddar cheese,
    grated
fresh parsley for garnish

Brown the onions and sugar gently in the margarine for 15 minutes, stirring occasionally. Stir in the flour and cook for 1 minute. Gradually stir in the stock, wine and seasoning. Partially cover and simmer for 30 minutes.

Lightly brush both sides of the bread slices with the oil and grill one side until pale golden. Turn the bread over, sprinkle with the cheese and grill until golden brown. Serve the soup in individual bowls with the bread slices floating on the top. Garnish with fresh parsley.

Brushing the bread with olive oil makes it wonderfully crisp when toasted under a hot grill, giving a good contrast to the smooth soup. Try any hard cheese of your choice for the croûtons: Gruyère or Parmesan impart wonderful strong flavours.

JANUARY

8

9

For Duchesse Potatoes, beat 1 egg into mashed potatoes, pipe into swirls and bake at 200°C/400°C/gas mark 6 for 30 minutes.

10

11

12

Lay pork chops on a bed of sliced apples, onions and mushrooms, pour on some apple juice, top with breadcrumbs and cheese and bake for 40 minutes.

14

To make apple wings as a garnish, halve an apple and lay it cut side down. Make 2 diagonal cuts and lift out a small wedge from the top. Continue to cut, following the lines of the first cut, until 2 wedges remain. Reshape the apple then gently separate the slices to form a wing shape.

Marinated Pork

4 pork chops
1 onion, finely chopped
1/2 tsp dried sage
1/2 tsp dried thyme
250 ml/8 fl oz dry cider
2 tbsp oil
1 tbsp butter

100 g/4 oz plain flour
salt and pepper
2 apples, peeled, cored and
   sliced
175 ml/6 fl oz chicken stock
1 tsp honey
1 tsp French mustard

Marinate the chops with the onion, herbs and cider for at least 2 hours, turning occasionally.

   Heat the oil and butter. Drain the chops and strain the marinade. Season the flour and use to dust the chops, then brown them in the hot butter and oil. Spread the apples in a greased ovenproof dish and place the chops on top. Fry the strained onion for 5 minutes until soft. Stir in the remaining flour and cook until just browned then stir in the marinade, stock, honey and mustard. Bring to the boil then pour over the chops. Cover and cook in a preheated oven at 180°C/350°F/gas mark 4 for 45 minutes. Serve with creamed potatoes and peas.

Marinating meat or fish in oil, cider or wine before cooking tenderises it, while the herbs give it extra flavour. Cover the meat and leave it in a cool place for at least 2 hours or overnight if possible.

15

19

Use beans or pulses as vegetables with grilled meats to provide healthy and colourful side dishes.

16

To save time, use canned beans, draining and rinsing them well before adding them to the pan.

20

17

21

18

Dried pulses should be soaked overnight in cold water then drained and rinsed thoroughly. To cook them, cover with fresh water, bring to the boil and simmer for about 1 hour until tender. Red kidney beans must be boiled vigorously for 15 minutes before simmering to destroy any toxins they contain.

Quick Goulash

1 onion, finely chopped
1 clove garlic, crushed
1 carrot, diced
2 courgettes, diced
2 tbsp olive oil
1 tbsp paprika
a pinch of freshly grated
    nutmeg
2 tbsp chopped fresh parsley

1 tbsp tomato purée
400 g/14 oz canned
    tomatoes
225 g/8 oz cooked white
    kidney beans
150 ml/¼ pt tomato juice
salt and pepper
2 tbsp soured cream or
    natural yoghurt

You can choose almost any type of beans for this dish: black, black eye, cannellini, haricot, lima or soy beans. The recipe also tastes good with chickpeas or lentils. Use a selection to give a variety of tastes and a wonderful range of colours.

Fry the onion, garlic, carrot and courgettes in the oil for 5 minutes until soft. Stir in the paprika, nutmeg, parsley and tomato purée and cook for 1 minute. Stir in the tomatoes, beans, tomato juice and seasoning, cover and cook for 15 minutes. Transfer to a warmed serving dish and drizzle the cream or yoghurt over the top. Serve with warm crusty bread and a salad of watercress and cabbage.

JANUARY

22

For a moist result, poach chicken half covered in water or stock with a few vegetables for about 1½ hours.

23

24

25

26

27

Fill tiny bottled peppers with a stuffing of minced meats and herbs and deep-fry for a delicious hot appetiser or snack.

28

You can also make Prawn or Crab Nuggets with finely chopped prawns or crab claws instead of chicken. Leave out the chilli if you do not like things too spicy, or substitute ¼ of a finely chopped green or red pepper.

Chicken Nuggets

450 g/1 lb cooked chicken,
   minced
175 g/6 oz breadcrumbs
1 tbsp butter
2 tbsp plain flour
150 ml/¼ pt milk
2 eggs, beaten

½ red or green chilli, seeded
   and chopped
1 spring onion, chopped
1 tbsp chopped fresh parsley
salt and pepper
oil for deep-frying

Mix together the chicken and half the breadcrumbs. Melt
the butter, stir in half the flour and cook for 1 minute.
Gradually stir in the milk and bring to the boil to make a
thick white sauce. Stir in the chicken and breadcrumbs with
the chilli, onion, parsley and seasoning and leave to cool.

Shape the mixture into 2.5 cm/1 in balls with floured
hands. Coat with beaten egg and roll in breadcrumbs.
Deep-fry in hot oil for about 5 minutes until golden brown.
Drain on kitchen paper and sprinkle lightly with salt
before serving.

You can either dip the
chicken balls into the egg
and turn with a fork or brush
them lightly with the egg
using a pastry brush. If you
have pressed the ingredients
together well when you
prepared them, they
should not break up.

Nuggets made with chicken
or fish can be served cold as
a cocktail snack, or hot with
chips and beans for supper.

JANUARY

29

31

Make sure you wash leeks thoroughly before slicing to remove any grit which lodges between the layers.

30

Use whatever shellfish you prefer for this recipe, but do make sure you buy them live and fresh and use them quickly. Whatever you choose - clams, mussels, scallops - scrub them well and soak them in several changes of fresh water. Discard any which do not close when tapped or do not open during cooking.

If you buy live lobster, cook it with the other shellfish until it turns red then remove and prepare it. Otherwise, use cooked lobster, fresh or frozen. Halve it lengthways, cut off the tail and remove the meat. Crack the claws and remove the meat as whole as possible. Discard the head. Buy raw prawns, if possible, for the sweetest flavour, but cooked prawns will also taste delicious.

Fish Stock

450 g/1 lb fish bones, skin
   and heads
1.75 litres/3 pts water
1 onion, sliced
1 carrot, sliced

1 bay leaf
6 black peppercorns
1 blade mace
1 sprig fresh thyme
1 slice lemon

Bring all the stock ingredients to the boil then simmer for 20 minutes. Strain the stock and discard the fish and vegetables.

Bouillabaisse

1 carrot, sliced
2 leeks, sliced
1 clove garlic, crushed
75 g/3 oz butter
a pinch of saffron
120 ml/4 fl oz dry white
   wine
225 g/8 oz canned tomatoes
450 g/1 lb cod or halibut
   fillets

450 g/1 lb mussels,
   scrubbed
450 g/1 lb small clams,
   scrubbed
8 small new potatoes,
   scrubbed
1 lobster, prepared
225 g/8 oz large peeled
   prawns
1 tbsp chopped fresh parsley

Fry the carrot, leeks and garlic in the butter for 5 minutes until soft. Add the saffron and wine and simmer for 5 minutes. Add the stock with the remaining ingredients except the lobster, prawns and parsley. Bring to the boil then simmer for about 15 minutes until the shellfish have opened and the potatoes are tender. Add the lobster and prawns, remove from the heat, cover and leave to stand for 5 minutes. Sprinkle with parsley and serve with garlic bread and a glass of lightly chilled dry white wine.

February

'The Summer hath his joys,
And Winter his delights.
Though Love and all his pleasures are but toys,
They shorten tedious nights.'

Thomas Campion

Spring may be just around
the corner – but still it snows and dismal weather can
make the shortest month seem like the longest. Brighten
those chilly days with fish pies and bakes and look closely
for the signs of spring to come: the tiny first shoots of the
daffodils pushing their way out of the damp dark earth,
the first early rhubarb for your favourite pies and
crumbles. And forget the cold at least for the 14th when
you can let the romantic in you run wild!

FEBRUARY

1

2

3 Chinese prawn crackers, fried briefly in hot oil, make a good side dish for a Chinese meal or a tasty cocktail snack.

4

5 Finish a Chinese meal with a glass of jasmine tea which you can buy in many supermarkets or delicatessens.

6

7

Remove the hard central core from the tomatoes with a sharp knife and cut them into wedges. Do not add them to the wok until the last minute so that they retain their shape and a slight crispness. Mangetout or mushrooms also go well with this sauce, with or without peppers.

Cantonese Beef

4 tbsp dark soy sauce
1 tbsp cornflour
1 tbsp dry sherry
1 tsp sugar
450 g/1 lb rump steak, cut
  into thin strips
2 large tomatoes, cut into
  wedges

2 tbsp salted black beans
2 tbsp water
4 tbsp oil
1 green pepper, cut into
  chunks
175 ml/6 fl oz beef stock
pepper

Salted black beans are available from delicatessens. Crush the beans in a small bowl with the back of a spoon to make a thick paste which gives a wonderful, authentic flavour.

Mix together the soy sauce, cornflour, sherry and sugar. Add the meat and set aside. Core the tomatoes and cut them into wedges. Crush the beans to a paste with the water. Heat the oil in a wok and stir-fry the pepper for 2 minutes then remove. Add the meat and marinade and stir-fry for 2 minutes. Add the bean paste and stock, bring to the boil and simmer for 5 minutes until slightly thickened. Add the peppers and tomatoes, season and stir-fry for 1 minute. Serve immediately with boiled rice.

8

12

9

13

Fold puréed canned peaches into whipped cream with a touch of cinnamon, chill and serve with ginger biscuits.

10

Wash and dry some rose petals. Dip in whisked egg white then caster sugar, leave to dry and use to decorate special desserts.

14

St Valentine's Day

11

To make the raspberry sauce, purée 225 g/8 oz fresh or frozen raspberries then rub them through a sieve to remove the pips. Stir in 25 g/1 oz icing sugar to sweeten. This is delicious with the Valentine Creams, poured over ice cream or swirled into yoghurt.

Valentine Creams

225 g/8 oz cream cheese
400 ml/14 fl oz whipping cream

75 g/3 oz icing sugar
2 tsp ground cinnamon

Whisk the cream cheese with 4 tbsp of cream until light and fluffy. Sift in the icing sugar and the cinnamon and blend well. Whip the remaining cream until stiff and fold it into the mixture. Line 4 moulds with damp muslin, spoon in the cream and press down to remove any air bubbles. Fold the muslin over the top and stand on a rack over a tray. Refrigerate for at least 8 hours. Turn out carefully, spoon over some raspberry sauce and serve garnished with candied rose petals.

Use moulds with small holes in the base so that any excess liquid can drain away during chilling. Line the moulds with dampened muslin or J-cloth, extending the material beyond the edges of the moulds.

FEBRUARY

15

16

17

An onion and tomato salad tastes good with Indian foods. Finely slice onions and mix with thin tomato wedges.

18

19

20

If you have time, prepare and cook curries in advance and reheat them, as this improves the flavour.

21

Spices are used in Indian foods to benefit the digestion as well as provide flavour and colour. Cook them before adding other ingredients to avoid a harsh taste. Peel ginger root before grating; do not use ground ginger. Wash your hands after preparing chillies as they contain an irritant.

Vegetable Curry

1 onion, finely chopped
1 green chilli pepper, seeded
   and finely chopped
1 small piece ginger root,
   grated

400 g/14 oz canned
   tomatoes, drained
225 g/8 oz cauliflower florets
150 ml/¼ pt vegetable stock
225 g/8 oz okra

2 cloves garlic, crushed
1 tbsp oil
½ tsp ground cumin
½ tsp ground turmeric
2 potatoes, diced
1 aubergine, cubed

100 g/4 oz roasted, unsalted
   cashew nuts
50 g/2 oz desiccated coconut
salt and pepper
4 tbsp natural yoghurt

Fry the onion, chilli, ginger and garlic in the oil for 5 minutes until soft. Stir in the spices and fry for 1 minute. Stir in the potatoes, aubergine and tomatoes, cover and cook for 10 minutes until the vegetables are almost tender. Add the cauliflower, stock and okra, cover and cook for 5 minutes until the vegetables are tender. Add the cashews, coconut and seasoning, heat through then transfer to a warmed serving dish. Drizzle the yoghurt over the top and serve with pilau rice.

You can use any of your favourite vegetables for this delicious curry. Try it with sliced courgettes, peas, carrots or broccoli. Remember to add first those vegetables that need the longest cooking, so they all finish cooking at the same time.

FEBRUARY

22

Basil has a strong flavour, so don't use too much. If you do not have fresh basil, stir in a little pesto sauce.

26

23

27

Most of the fat in chicken is contained in the skin, so remove this before or after cooking for a healthier meal.

24

28/29

25

Use a very sharp knife to peel limes, lemons or oranges so that you remove all the white pith, which can be bitter. Remove the pithy centre and push out any seeds. Slice as thinly as possible, retaining the shape of the fruit.

Lime-Roasted Chicken

4 chicken breasts
salt and pepper
4 limes
2 tsp white wine vinegar

5 tbsp olive oil
2 tsp chopped fresh basil
1 sprig fresh basil

Rub the chicken with salt and pepper, place in an ovenproof dish and set aside. Use a lemon zester to pare away thin strips of rind from 2 limes then cut them in half and squeeze the juice. Mix the lime juice and rind with the wine vinegar and 4 tbsp of oil, pour over the chicken, cover and refrigerate for at least 4 hours, overnight if possible, basting occasionally.

Baste the chicken thoroughly then bake in a preheated oven at 190°C/375°F/gas mark 5 for 30 minutes until tender. Meanwhile, peel and slice the remaining limes.

Heat the remaining oil and fry the lime slices and basil for 1 minute until beginning to soften. Arrange the chicken on a warmed serving platter, pour over the sauce and garnish with the basil sprig. Serve with creamed potatoes and steamed mangetout lightly tossed in butter.

Vary the recipe using lemons and thyme instead of lime and basil for a slightly sharper taste. Always make sure chicken is thoroughly cooked by spearing the thickest point of the thigh with a skewer. If the juices run clear, the chicken is ready.

March

'When daffodils begin to peer,
With heigh! the doxy, over the dale,
Why, then comes in the sweet o' the year;
For the red blood reigns in the winter's pale.'
William Shakespeare

THE WINDS may still be
strong and the rain squally, but they toss the yellow
heads of the daffodils and scatter the now-green grass
with early blossom. The new life of spring begins to
burst on every side. Days grow longer, the clocks move
on to Summer Time and Easter is approaching. New life
is breathing in the kitchen, too, with the new vegetables
of the season, crisp and tender, ready for lighter
dishes to come.

MARCH

1 St David's Day

Leeks are a must today! Slice them into rings, fry them in a little butter and chicken stock and serve with grilled lamb chops.

2

3

4

5

6

Make Breton pancakes with buckwheat flour and serve them with a ham and cheese filling and a mug of dry cider.

7

Pancakes can be filled with almost anything you fancy, then rolled up and baked or simply served as they are to create a perfect snack, lunch or dessert. Try cottage cheese and walnuts, mushrooms in sauce, prawns, cooked smoked haddock with chopped tomato and onion, cherries with fromage frais.

Pancakes

100 g/4 oz plain flour
a pinch of salt
1 egg, beaten
300 ml/¹/₂ pt milk
1 tbsp vegetable oil

juice and pared
  rind of 1 lemon
juice and pared rind of 1
  orange

Mix the flour and salt and make a well in the centre. Beat the egg and milk and stir it into the flour then beat to a smooth batter. Heat a little oil in a pancake pan and pour in some batter, tilting the pan so that the batter spreads as thinly as possible. Cook until brown on the base, then turn or toss and cook the other side. Layer the pancakes between sheets of greaseproof paper and keep them warm while you fry the remaining batter. Garnish with the citrus rind and serve with the juice.

The best way to pare thin strips from citrus fruits is to use a lemon zester, otherwise use a very sharp knife and cut the rind into strips. Make sure you cut off any white pith as this tastes bitter.

MARCH

8

12

9

Mix poached, flaked plaice with prawns, chopped hard-boiled eggs, parsley and white sauce, top with mashed potatoes and bake.

13

10

14

Try making turnovers with meat, chicken or vegetables for a lunch box or a picnic on a warm spring day.

11

Use whichever type of mushrooms you prefer: chestnut, large, button or oyster, for example. You can make mushroom turnovers with 225 g/8 oz mushrooms and 50 g/2 oz breadcrumbs stirred into a white sauce made with 25 g/1 oz butter, 25 g/1 oz flour and 120 ml/4 fl oz each milk and vegetable stock.

Plaice Turnovers

4 plaice fillets, skinned
salt and pepper
6 tbsp milk
100 g/4 oz button
    mushrooms, sliced
2 tbsp butter
juice of 1 lemon

3 tbsp coarsely ground
    hazelnuts
375 g/12 oz frozen puff
    pastry
1 egg, beaten
1 tsp poppy seeds

Season the plaice, roll up and secure with cocktail sticks.
Place in an ovenproof dish with the milk, cover and poach in
a preheated oven at 180°C/350°F/gas mark 4 for 10
minutes. Drain, remove the cocktail sticks and leave to
cool. Cook the mushrooms, butter and lemon juice in a
small pan for about 5 minutes. Leave to cool then stir in
the hazelnuts. Roll out the pastry and cut into 4 x 15 cm/
6 in circles. Place a fish roll on each one and divide the
stuffing mixture between them. Brush the edges with
beaten egg and pinch them together to seal. Brush all over
with egg and sprinkle with poppy seeds. Bake the
turnovers on a greased baking sheet in a preheated oven at
200°C/400°F/gas mark 6 for 25 minutes
until puffed and golden. Serve
with a green salad and
potatoes glazed
in butter.

To seal a turnover, make
sure you have brushed the
edges well with beaten egg.
Pull the pastry edges up and
over the filling and pinch the
edges together firmly.
Alternatively you can use a
pastry press.

MARCH

15

Smother slices of braising steak with sliced onions and a little stock, cover and braise in a low oven for 2 hours.

19

16

20

Mince 750g/1¹/₂ lb steak and mix with 1 egg, 100 g/4 oz breadcrumbs, 1 chopped onion and seasoning to make tasty meatballs.

17 **St Patrick's Day**

21

18

To make Irish Griddle Scones, knead together 100 g/4 oz self-raising flour, ¹/₂ tsp salt, 40 g/1¹/₂ oz butter, ¹/₂ tsp freshly grated nutmeg, 1 egg and 6 tbsp milk. Make into 2 flat rounds 1 cm/¹/₂ in thick, cut into 6 triangles and cook on a greased griddle for about 5 minutes each side.

Traditionally drunk with oysters fresh from the sea, Guinness is synonymous with Ireland, and they say that nowhere but in Ireland does it taste exactly as it should. It gives a wonderful rich flavour and tenderises meat during the long slow cooking.

Beef in Guinness

750 g/1¹/₂ lb chuck steak	salt and pepper
225 g/8 oz carrots	¹/₂ tsp chopped fresh basil
3 tbsp oil	150 ml/¹/₄ pt Guinness
2 onions, chopped	1 tsp honey
3 tbsp plain flour	150 ml/¹/₄ pt beef stock

Cut the steak into about 12 x 2.5 cm/1 in thick pieces. Trim the carrots into pieces about the size of your little finger. Heat the oil and fry the onions for 5 minutes until soft then use a slotted spoon to transfer then to a shallow greased ovenproof dish. Season the flour, dip in the meat and fry in the oil until browned then transfer to the casserole with the carrots. Stir the flour into the pan and cook for 1 minute. Stir in the basil and Guinness, bring to the boil and simmer for 1 minute. Stir in the honey and stock, return to the boil and pour over the meat. Cover and bake in a preheated oven at 160°C/325°F/gas mark 3 for 1¹/₂ hours. Serve with mashed or boiled potatoes and lightly steamed cabbage.

22

Dip onion rings into a thick flour and water batter, fry until crisp and serve with grilled meat and ratatouille.

26

23

27

24

Garlic is very popular in Mediterranean cooking. It gives a wonderful flavour and is also very good for you.

28

25

Aubergines contain bitter juices which must be extracted before you use them. You can either halve them and score the flesh or slice them thickly. Sprinkle generously with salt and stand them in a colander so that the juices can drain off. Rinse well under running water and pat dry before use.

Ratatouille

2 aubergines
salt
4 tbsp olive oil
2 Spanish onions, thinly
   sliced
4 courgettes, sliced
1 red pepper, chopped

1 green pepper, chopped
2 tbsp chopped fresh basil
1 large clove garlic, crushed
800 g/1 lb 10 oz canned
   tomatoes
pepper
150 ml/^{1}/$_4$ pt dry white wine

Halve the aubergines and score the cut sides diagonally
with a sharp knife. Sprinkle with salt and leave to
stand for 30 minutes. Rinse and pat dry then chop
roughly. Heat the oil and fry the onions for
5 minutes until soft and beginning to brown.
Stir in the courgettes and peppers and cook
gently for 5 minutes. Remove from the pan
and set aside. Add the aubergines to the
pan and cook for 8 minutes until
beginning to brown, then add the other
vegetables and all the remaining
ingredients except the wine to the
pan. Bring to the boil then simmer
for 15 minutes until thickened.
Add the wine and cook for a
further 15 minutes.
Serve hot or cold.

To prepare peppers, halve
them and remove the seeds
and white pith then chop or
slice the flesh as required.
Onions need to be peeled
and halved then sliced with a
sharp knife. Wash
courgettes, trim the ends
and slice neatly into rings.

29

31

30

To skin tomatoes, cut a small cross into the skins and plunge them into boiling water for 10 seconds then into cold water. The skins should peel away easily with a sharp knife.

Indian basmati rice has an excellent flavour and stays moist and separate. You can buy ground saffron or saffron strands. Crush saffron strands in a little boiling water before adding them to the dish.

Saffron Chicken

2 tbsp olive oil
1 small chicken, jointed
salt and pepper
1 onion, finely chopped
1 clove garlic, crushed
2 tsp paprika
8 tomatoes, skinned and
    chopped

300 g/11 oz long-grain rice
900 ml/1½ pts boiling water
a large pinch of saffron
    strands or ¼ tsp ground
    saffron
175 g/6 oz frozen peas
2 tbsp chopped fresh parsley

Before you start the recipe, joint the chicken. Cut the chicken in half lengthways down the breast bone and through the backbone. Cut the halves in half again, slitting between the leg joint diagonally up and around the breast joint. Cut away the drumsticks from the leg thigh joint and the wings from the breast joint to make 8 pieces. Remove the skin by pulling and cutting with a sharp knife.

Heat the oil in a large flameproof casserole dish and fry the chicken pieces for about 5 minutes until browned. Season, remove from the dish and set aside. Add the onion and garlic to the dish and fry gently for 5 minutes until soft but not browned. Stir in the paprika and fry for 30 seconds. Add the tomatoes and cook for 10 minutes until slightly thickened. Stir in the rice, water, saffron and chicken. Bring to the boil then cover and simmer gently for about 15 minutes. Add the peas and parsley and simmer for a further 5 minutes until the rice is tender and the liquid has been absorbed.

April

'When well-apparelled April on the heel
Of limping Winter treads.'
William Shakespeare

SPRING is here at last!
Refreshed by April showers, the garden begins to
blossom and new vegetables appear almost daily. April
has a wonderful variety – the weather varies from cold and
blowy to almost summery and mild. In the kitchen, too,
cooks offer warming fish dishes on colder days then
tempt you into summer with the earliest broad beans
and salad vegetables.

APRIL

1   **April Fool's Day**   The oldest April fool breakfast is the empty egg shell upside down in its cup and beautifully served with hot toast.

5

2

6   Toss lightly steamed broccoli in 2 tbsp olive oil and 2 tsp anchovy paste until hot for an unusual side dish.

3

7

4

Make chilli flowers from small green or red chillies to decorate oriental dishes. Slit the chillies lengthways from the tip, leaving about 2.5 cm/1 in of the stalk end intact. Scrape out the seeds and ribs. Stand the chillies in a bowl of iced water for 1 hour until they curl into flowers.

Spicy Noodles

12 Chinese dried
    mushrooms
225 g/8 oz Chinese egg
    noodles
5 tbsp oil
4 carrots, thinly sliced
225 g/8 oz broccoli florets
1 clove garlic

4 spring onions, diagonally
    sliced
1 tsp chilli sauce
4 tbsp soy sauce
4 tbsp rice wine or dry
    sherry
2 tsp cornflour

Soak the mushrooms in warm water for about 30 minutes.
Meanwhile, cook the noodles in boiling salted water for
about 5 minutes. Drain, rinse under hot water and drain
again. Toss with 1 tbsp of oil. Blanch the carrots and
broccoli in boiling water for 2 minutes. Drain and rinse
under cold water. Drain the mushrooms, discard the stems
and slice the caps. Heat the remaining oil with the garlic in
a wok then remove the garlic. Add the carrots and broccoli
and stir-fry for 1 minute. Add the mushrooms and spring
onions and stir-fry for 2 minutes. Mix together the chilli
sauce, soy sauce, wine or sherry and cornflour. Pour over
the vegetables and stir-fry until the sauce clears. Add the
noodles and toss together
until heated through.

You can use any type of egg
noodles for this dish, or use
rice noodles. Both are
available dried in various
thicknesses in supermarkets
or delicatessens. In China
they are a symbol of
longevity and are often
served at birthday parties as
a wish for long life.

8

For a tasty buffet dish, purée some light pâté and whipped cream until soft and pipe it into little rolls of ham.

12

9

13

To make sweet eggs, colour tiny pieces of almond paste with food colouring and roll in mixed spice for a speckled effect.

10

14

11

This recipe makes a perfect starter, snack or canapé. It is delicious served cold, so makes an attractive dish for a picnic or buffet table. You do not have to stick to hen's eggs. Quail, duck, goose or bantam eggs work equally well.

Stuffed Eggs

4 eggs
225 g/8 oz cooked ham,
   minced
4 tbsp grated mild cheese
4 tbsp soured cream
2 tsp made mustard

salt and pepper
2 tsp chopped fresh dill or
   chives
3 tbsp breadcrumbs
25 g/1 oz butter, melted
1 sprig fresh parsley

Make a small hole into the larger end of each egg and lower them gently into boiling water. As the water returns to the boil, roll the eggs around for 2 minutes to help set the yolks. Cook for a further 8 minutes. Drain and rinse then leave in cold water until ready to shell. Shell the eggs, halve them lengthways and remove the yolks. Mix the yolks with all the remaining ingredients except the breadcrumbs, butter and parsley. Pipe or spoon the mixture back into the egg whites. Sprinkle over the breadcrumbs and drizzle with melted butter. Place under a preheated grill for about 3 minutes until crisp and golden brown. Serve garnished with parsley.

15

16

Brush a whole, cleaned sea bream with oil, season with dried oregano and bake at 180°C/350°F/gas mark 4 for 25 minutes.

17

18

There are many different varieties of lettuce now available, from the familiar cos, Webbs and iceberg to the more unusual curly endive, radicchio and lamb's lettuce. Try a selection to find your favourites. The darker-leaved varieties tend to be slightly bitter, so use them sparingly.

19

20

Scatter cubes of your favourite hard cheese over a layer of tomato slices and dress with olive oil and pepper.

21 **Queen Elizabeth II's birthday**

Spring Salad

400 g/14 oz cottage cheese
1 carrot, coarsely grated
8 radishes, coarsely grated
2 spring onions, thinly
    sliced
salt and pepper

1 tsp chopped fresh dill or
    marjoram
150 ml/¼ pt soured cream
    or thick yoghurt
selection of lettuce leaves
4 sprigs fresh dill

Grate the vegetables on the coarse side of the grater to create short strips which will absorb the flavours of the salad while retaining their crispness.
If you are making a larger quantity, it may be quicker to use a food processor.

Strain excess liquid from the cottage cheese while you prepare the vegetables. Mix together all the ingredients except the lettuce leaves and dill sprigs and chill for about 20 minutes. To serve, arrange a selection of lettuce leaves and a mound of salad on individual plates and garnish with sprigs of dill. Serve with thinly sliced rye, wholemeal or French bread and butter.

APRIL

22

26 Fry diced cooked lamb in butter with chopped bacon, onion, parsley, fried potato and Worcester sauce; top with fried eggs.

23 St George's Day

27

24 Scoop the insides out of cooked jacket potatoes, mix with butter and egg, pile back in the shells and bake until golden.

28

25 Make another delicious lamb stuffing by frying 1 small chopped onion in a little butter then mixing it with the grated rind and juice of 1 orange, 50 g/2 oz breadcrumbs, 75 g/3 oz mixed sultanas, raisins and currants and a little rosemary and thyme, salt and pepper.

Stuffed Lamb

half breast of lamb
1 onion
salt and pepper
225 g/8 oz breadcrumbs
25 g/1 oz shredded suet
1/2 tsp dried marjoram

1/2 tsp dried thyme
grated rind of 1/2 lemon
1 egg
1 tbsp plain flour
2 sprigs fresh parsley

Bone the lamb. Place the bones in a saucepan with half the onion and some salt and pepper. Cover with water, bring to the boil, skim, cover and simmer for 30 minutes. Strain and reserve the stock. Finely chop the remaining onion and mix it with the breadcrumbs, suet, herbs, lemon rind, salt, pepper, egg and 2 tbsp of stock. Spread the stuffing over the lamb, roll up and tie firmly with string. Bake in a greased roasting tin in a preheated oven at 200°C/400°F/ gas mark 6 for 1 hour. Transfer the meat to a warmed serving dish and keep it warm. Drain off any excess fat from the tin, stir in the flour and cook for 1 minute. Stir in 250 ml/8 fl oz of stock, bring to the boil, stirring, and boil for 3 minutes. Strain into a gravy boat. Garnish the lamb with parsley and serve with new potatoes and courgettes.

For a deliciously creamy and unusual sauce, use slightly less stock for the gravy and mix in 4 tbsp redcurrant jelly and 4 tbsp cream, seasoning to taste. Slice the lamb, arrange the slices on a warmed serving dish and pour over the sauce to serve.

29

30

Salmon steaks make a great meal simply brushed with melted butter and crushed garlic and grilled until tender.

The best way to cook fresh salmon is to poach it in a court bouillon. Finely chop 2 carrots, 1 onion, 2 sticks celery and 2 shallots and mix with 1 bay leaf, 3 parsley stalks, 2 sprigs fresh thyme, 2 tbsp lemon juice, 300 ml/½ pt dry white wine and 900 ml/1½ pts water. Cover and simmer for 15 minutes. Meanwhile, cut the fins and gills off the cleaned fish, cut an inverted V into the tail and wash it well. Strain the court bouillon over the fish in a buttered ovenproof dish or fish kettle, cover and poach in a preheated oven at 180°C/350°F/gas mark 4 for about 8 minutes per 450 g/1 lb until the fish flakes when tested with a fork.

Leave to cool in the court bouillon then remove the fish. Snip the skin just below the head and above the tail and carefully peel off the skin. Snip the backbone below the head and above the tail then split the fish along the backbone with a sharp knife. Ease the bone out from the back without breaking the fish. Salmon steaks can be poached in the same way.

You can add a little chopped dill to the flan if you wish. An attractive feathery herb, it is often used with fish dishes because of its delicate flavour. Dill seeds are also available but these have a stronger taste.

Salmon Flan

75 g/6 oz frozen puff pastry
2 tsp cornflour
150 ml/$^1/_4$ pt milk
75 g/6 oz cooked fresh
  or canned salmon

salt and pepper
1 tbsp butter (optional)
1 egg, beaten
4 sprigs fresh dill

Roll out the pastry and use to line a greased 20 cm/8 in flan dish. Mix the cornflour with a little milk. Bring the remaining milk to the boil, stir into the cornflour mixture then return to the pan and cook for 1 minute, stirring constantly. Season with salt and pepper. Mix the butter into the fresh salmon or drain the canned salmon and flake the fish, removing any bones or skin. Remove the sauce from the heat and beat in the egg then fold in the salmon and spoon the mixture into the pastry case. Bake in a preheated oven at 190°C/375°F/gas mark 5 for 40 minutes. Serve garnished with dill sprigs with a crisp salad and wholemeal bread or baked potatoes and petits pois.

May

'And the May month flaps its glad green leaves like wings,
Delicate-filmed as new-spun silk,'

Thomas Hardy

Spring is flourishing, the summer buds are shooting and the first tender young asparagus brings its delicate flavour into the kitchen. Lightness and softness are the keynotes: the newest vegetables are meltingly tender; the fruits begin to soften and ripen, with fresh-skinned apricots and melons ripe from Spain. Once May Day is over, summer is just a step away and you can cast away your winter coats.

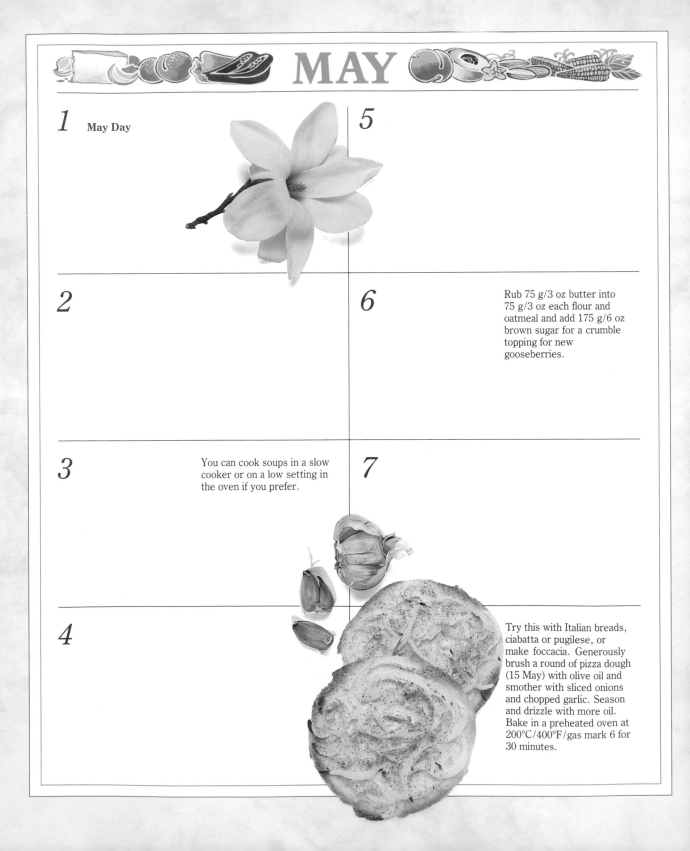

MAY

1   May Day

5

2

6   Rub 75 g/3 oz butter into 75 g/3 oz each flour and oatmeal and add 175 g/6 oz brown sugar for a crumble topping for new gooseberries.

3   You can cook soups in a slow cooker or on a low setting in the oven if you prefer.

7

4   Try this with Italian breads, ciabatta or pugilese, or make foccacia. Generously brush a round of pizza dough (15 May) with olive oil and smother with sliced onions and chopped garlic. Season and drizzle with more oil. Bake in a preheated oven at 200°C/400°F/gas mark 6 for 30 minutes.

Minestrone means 'big soup'. For a thinner soup, omit the pasta and reduce the amount of vegetables.

Minestrone

100 g/4 oz dried white cannellini beans
1.2 litres/2 pts vegetable stock
2 tbsp olive oil
1 onion, finely chopped
1 clove garlic, crushed
1 stick celery, thinly sliced
2 carrots, diced
50 g/2 oz green beans

100 g/4 oz spring greens, shredded
1 courgette, diced
100 g/4 oz tomatoes, skinned and diced
1 bay leaf
50 g/2 oz pasta shells
salt and pepper
1 tbsp chopped fresh basil
1 tbsp chopped fresh parsley

Soak the beans overnight in the stock. Heat the oil and fry the onion and garlic for 5 minutes until soft but not browned. Add the vegetables and fry for 5 minutes until soft. Add the beans and stock, the tomatoes, bay leaf, pasta and seasoning. Bring to the boil, cover and simmer for 1 hour until the beans are tender, stirring occasionally. Stir in the basil and parsley and heat through for 5 minutes. Serve with crusty bread.

There are many different recipes for minestrone, but they all make a substantial soup. You can substitute almost any vegetables of your choice, according to what is available. Any small shape of pasta is fine, or you can use broken pieces of spaghetti or long-grain rice.

MAY

8

Take advantage of the young carrots now available. Slice into strips and cook briefly so they are sweet and crisp.

9

10

11

12

13

To make herb oils to dress salads, place sprigs of basil, rosemary or bay in a bottle, fill with olive oil, seal and store for 4 weeks.

14

There is no limit to omelette ingredients! Try prawns, sweetcorn, sliced mushrooms, grated cheese, diced black pudding, chopped fresh herbs, diced potatoes, flaked salmon or salami. If the omelette is thick, do not fold it in half, but place it under a hot grill until golden brown.

Ham and Pepper Omelette

3 eggs, beaten
2 tbsp milk
salt and pepper
25 g/1 oz green pepper,
    chopped

2 tomatoes, skinned, seeded
    and chopped
50 g/2 oz ham, diced
1 tbsp vegetable oil

Beat the eggs, milk and seasoning. Heat the oil and fry the pepper for 5 minutes until soft. Stir in the tomatoes and ham and heat through for 1 minute. Pour in the egg mixture and stir well until it begins to cook. As the egg begins to set, lift it and tilt the pan to allow the uncooked egg to run underneath. When the underside is cooked and the top is still slightly creamy, fold the omelette in half and serve at once with a crisp salad and crusty bread.

Green and red peppers, courgettes and any type of ham make excellent additions to omelettes. Chop them finely or coarsely, as you prefer, and fry them until they are just beginning to soften so they still have a slight crunch.

15

To obtain the right temperature of warm water when using yeast, use half boiling water and half tap water.

19

16

20

17

Grill pizza toppings on French bread for a quick snack or tasty supper.

21

18

Other topping ingredients include Italian hams and sausages, tuna, clams, capers, courgettes, olives or Ricotta cheese. To make a calzone, brush the dough with olive oil and cover half with chopped ham and boiled egg, and cubes of Mozzarella. Fold in half, seal and brush with oil before baking.

Pizza Dough

15 g/¹/₂ oz fresh yeast
*   or 1 tsp dried*
¹/₂ tsp sugar
175 ml/6 fl oz warm water
225 g/8 oz strong plain
*   flour*
a pinch of salt
2 tbsp olive oil

Cream the yeast and sugar in a small bowl, stir in the water and leave to stand for about 10 minutes until frothy. Sift the flour and salt into a bowl and make a well in the centre. Add the oil and yeast mixture and work the flour into the liquid to form a firm dough. Turn on to a floured surface and knead until smooth and elastic. Place in a lightly oiled bowl, cover and leave to stand in a warm place for 1 hour until doubled in size. Knead again and flatten the dough into a 25 cm/10 in circle.

Italian Pizza

2 tbsp olive oil
1 onion, chopped
1 clove garlic, crushed
400 g/14 oz canned tomatoes
1 tbsp tomato purée
¹/₂ tsp dried oregano
¹/₂ tsp chopped fresh basil
1 tsp sugar
salt and pepper

100 g/4 oz Mozzarella
*   cheese, grated*
25 g/1 oz Parmesan cheese,
*   grated*
¹/₂ red pepper, sliced
¹/₂ green pepper, sliced
7 black olives, stoned
50 g/2 oz canned anchovies,
*   drained*

Heat the oil and fry the onion and garlic for 5 minutes until soft but not browned. Add the tomatoes and juice, tomato purée, herbs, sugar, salt and pepper. Bring to the boil and simmer until thick and smooth, stirring occasionally. Leave to cool. Spread the sauce over the dough, sprinkle over half the cheese then arrange the peppers, olives and anchovies on top. Sprinkle with the remaining cheese and bake in a preheated oven at 200°C/ 400°F/gas mark 6 for 20 minutes.

22

When cooking rice, fill a measuring jug with rice up to 300 ml/¹/₂ pt for 4 people and use twice the volume of water.

26

23

27

24

Soak dried fruits in boiling water for about 10 minutes to plump them up then drain well before use.

28

25

As an alternative dressing, whisk together 4 tbsp dry sherry, 3 tbsp olive oil, 2 tbsp white wine vinegar, 1 tsp lemon juice and some salt and pepper. Flavour dressings with a sprinkling of chopped fresh herbs if you wish.

Rice and Nut Salad

2 tbsp olive oil
2 tbsp lemon juice
salt and pepper
100 g/4 oz sultanas, soaked
50 g/2 oz currants, soaked
275 g/10 oz cooked brown
    rice
75 g/3 oz almonds, chopped
50 g/2 oz walnuts, chopped

50 g/2 oz cashew nuts,
    chopped
425 g/15 oz peach slices in
    natural juice, drained
    and chopped
1/4 cucumber, cubed
100 g/4 oz cooked red kidney
    beans
6 black olives, stoned

Put the olive oil, lemon juice, salt and pepper in a screw-top jar and shake vigorously until thickened. Mix together the soaked fruits, rice, nuts, peaches, cucumber, beans and olives. Pour over the dressing and toss thoroughly. Serve on bed of shredded crisp lettuce or endive.

You can substitute apricots or kiwi fruit for the peaches if you prefer and, of course, you can use fresh fruit if they are available. Whatever you choose, this makes a highly nutritious salad which is perfect for a lunch or supper dish.

MAY

29

31

30

Feta cheese is a soft white Greek cheese made with ewes' or goats' milk. You can substitute a creamy cheese such as Ricotta or even a crumbled mild English cheese such as Caerphilly for this recipe if you prefer.

To prepare spinach, tear off the stalks by holding the leaves firmly and pulling the stems backwards. Wash the leaves thoroughly, drain well, then shred them with a sharp knife. If you use frozen spinach, simply heat through the thawed spinach with the softened onions then leave to cool.

You can make a delicious Spinach and Onion Flan using the same onion and spinach mixture. Line a flan dish with shortcrust pastry and spread it with the onion mixture. Beat 3 eggs with 4 tbsp single cream and 4 tbsp milk and pour over the flan. Season with freshly grated nutmeg and bake in a preheated oven at 200°C/400°F/ gas mark 6 for 30 minutes.

Spinach and Feta Pie

225 g/8 oz filo pastry
450 g/1 lb spinach
2 tbsp olive oil
1 onion, finely chopped
1 tbsp chopped fresh dill

3 eggs, beaten
100 g/4 oz feta cheese
salt and pepper
50 g/2 oz butter, melted

Cut the pastry to fit the size of your baking dish, then keep it covered with a damp cloth. Prepare the spinach. Heat the oil and fry the onion for 5 minutes until soft. Add the spinach and stir for 5 minutes over a medium heat then increase the heat to evaporate any moisture. Leave to cool then mix in the dill, eggs, cheese, salt and pepper. Brush the baking dish with melted butter. Brush 8 layers of pastry with butter and lay them in the bottom of the dish. Spread with the filling, then cover with the remaining pastry, brushing each one with melted butter and scoring the top into diamond shapes. Sprinkle with water and bake in a preheated oven at 190°C/375°F/gas mark 5 for 40 minutes until crisp and golden. Leave to stand for 10 minutes then cut into wedges and serve with crisp lettuce leaves.

Filo pastry is available frozen in packets, ready rolled into thin sheets. It is easy to handle, but must be covered with a damp cloth to keep it moist while you are preparing the dish. Brush lightly with sunflower oil rather than butter if you prefer.

June

'A noise like of a hidden brook,
In the leafy month of June,
That to the sleeping woods all night
Singeth a quiet tune.'
Samuel Taylor Coleridge

EARLY summer – such a
wonderful season as the weather warms, the evenings
grow longer and the colour green seems to have more
shades than you could possibly have imagined. Variety is
paramount. You can scarcely choose which salad
vegetables to buy, they all look so crisp and delicious.
And at every turn something new appears in the garden
and in the kitchen. This is a time for experiments – try
them all!

JUNE

1

2

Groundnut oil is perfect for stir-frying as it has a mild taste and can be heated to high temperatures.

3

4

5

Mix 100 g/4 oz chopped prawns, 50 g/2 oz butter, 1/2 tsp curry paste and 1 tbsp chopped parsley, spread on toast and grill lightly.

6

7

Chinese rice wine is made from glutinous rice, yeast and spring water. It is widely used in China for cooking and drinking. You can buy it in delicatessens or oriental supermarkets and it should be stored tightly corked at room temperature. You can substitute a dry sherry.

Quick-Fried Prawns

900 g/2 lb cooked prawns
2 cloves garlic, crushed
2.5 cm/1 in piece ginger
  root, finely chopped
1 tbsp chopped fresh
  coriander

3 tbsp groundnut oil
1 tbsp rice wine or dry
  sherry
2 tbsp light soy sauce
4 spring onions, sliced

Shell the prawns, leaving on the tails. Place them in a bowl
with all the remaining ingredients except the spring onions
and leave to marinate for 30 minutes. Heat a wok and add
the prawns and marinade. Stir-fry for a few minutes until
heated through then serve sprinkled with
spring onion rings.

You can also use
half prawns and half
shelled scallops for
this recipe.

JUNE

8

9

10

Mix Ricotta cheese with chopped fresh basil and use it to fill bottled cherry peppers. Serve as cocktail nibbles.

11

12

13

Liven up soft scoop ice cream by pouring over some fruit purée and sprinkling with chopped nuts.

14

Serve the salad with mortadella, prosciutto or salami, crusty bread and dry white wine. Make Pepper and Pasta Salad by frying 2 sliced peppers with 1 sliced onion, 2 sliced courgettes, a clove of garlic and 2 skinned tomatoes. Mix with cooked pasta spirals, season and dress with oil and vinegar.

Pepper Sunburst

2 red peppers
2 green peppers
2 yellow peppers
6 tbsp oil
1 tbsp white wine vinegar
1 small clove garlic, crushed
a pinch of salt

a pinch of cayenne pepper
a pinch of sugar
2 hard-boiled eggs
18 black olives, stoned
1 tbsp chopped fresh
  coriander

Halve the peppers and remove the seeds. Press them down to flatten them. Brush the skin side with a little oil and grill until the skins begin to char and split. Place the peppers in a loosely-tied plastic bag and leave for 15 minutes. Whisk together the remaining oil, wine vinegar, garlic, salt, cayenne pepper and sugar. Cut the eggs into wedges. Remove the peppers from the bag, peel away the skin and cut the flesh into thick strips. Arrange on a serving plate with the eggs and olives. Sprinkle with the coriander and spoon over the dressing. Chill for 1 hour before serving.

You can use any colours of pepper for this salad, and roast them in a hot oven instead of under the grill. To make the salad in double-quick time, use bottled or canned peppers, drain them thoroughly and slice them into strips.

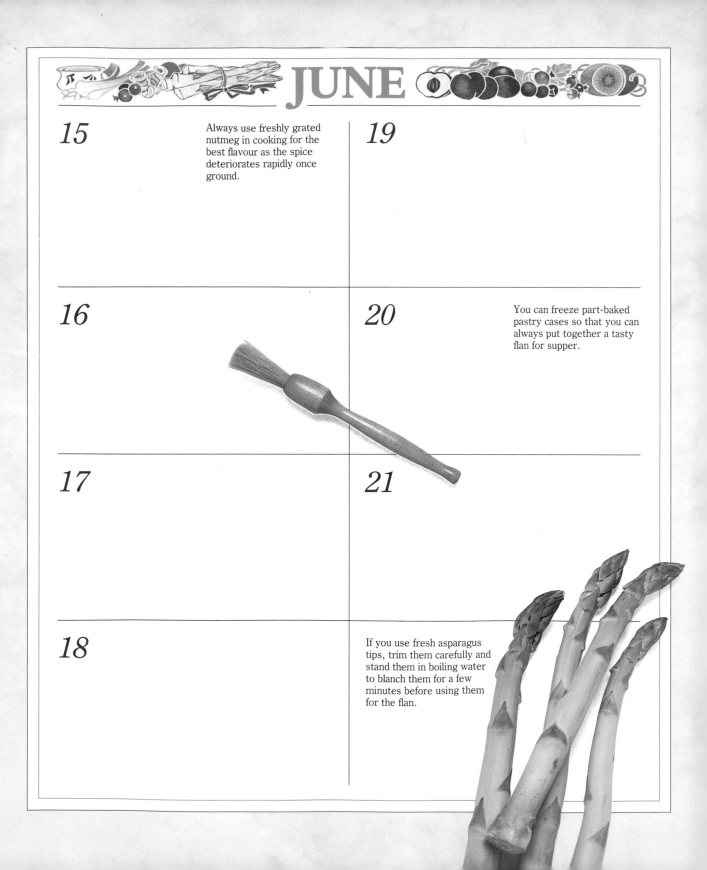

JUNE

15

Always use freshly grated nutmeg in cooking for the best flavour as the spice deteriorates rapidly once ground.

16

17

18

19

20

You can freeze part-baked pastry cases so that you can always put together a tasty flan for supper.

21

If you use fresh asparagus tips, trim them carefully and stand them in boiling water to blanch them for a few minutes before using them for the flan.

Asparagus Quiche

75 g/3 oz butter
50 g/2 oz lard
225 g/8 oz plain flour
3 tbsp water
3 eggs
300 ml/¹/₂ pt single cream
a pinch of freshly grated
    nutmeg
salt and pepper
2 tbsp plain flour

225 g/8 oz canned
    asparagus tips
75 g/3 oz green olives,
    stoned
1 onion, chopped and fried
    in butter
50 g/2 oz Cheddar cheese,
    grated
1 tbsp grated Parmesan
    cheese

Any hard cheese is suitable for this flan. Try to buy fresh Parmesan and grate it yourself for the best flavour. Ready-grated tubs of Parmesan do not taste the same.

Rub 50 g/2 oz of butter and the lard into the flour and mix with enough water to make a pastry. Roll out and use to line a 25 cm/10 in flan ring. Cover with greaseproof paper, fill with baking beans and bake in a preheated oven at 190°C/375°F/gas mark 5 for 10 minutes. Remove the beans and paper. Whisk the eggs, cream, nutmeg and seasoning. Mix a little of the mixture with the flour then stir it into the cream. Arrange the asparagus, olives and onion in the pastry case, pour over the cream and sprinkle with the cheeses. Dot with the remaining butter and bake for 25 minutes. Reduce the heat to 180°C/350°F/gas mark 4 for a further 15 minutes until the quiche is golden.

JUNE

22

26

23

Add 3 tbsp of rum to mango purée to give extra flavour for special occasions.

27

Blend together 4 tbsp gin, 4 tbsp coconut cream, 4 strawberries and 2 scoops crushed ice for an exotic summer cocktail.

24 Midsummer Day

28

25

When you are preparing fruit for a salad, always slice or cut it to show its most attractive side. Slice kiwi fruit crosswise to reveal their stunning colour and pattern. Slice star fruit thinly and maintain its lovely shape. Cut passion fruit in half with a zig-zag pattern.

Exotic Fruit Salad

3 ripe peaches
3 kiwi fruits
1 star fruit
100 g/4 oz ripe strawberries

2 ripe mangoes
juice of ¹/₂ lime
150 g/5 oz redcurrants
a few strawberry leaves

Raspberries, apricots, cherries, plums, blackberries, grapes, pineapple, passion fruit and guava are all suitable for this wonderful salad.

Plunge the peaches into boiling water for a few seconds then carefully peel away the skin using a sharp knife. Cut them in half, remove the stones and slice the flesh. Peel and slice the kiwi fruits. Trim and slice the star fruit. Leave the stems on the strawberries and halve them lengthways. Arrange the fruit on a serving platter. Peel and stone the mangoes, chop the flesh and purée it with the lime juice and half the redcurrants then rub the purée through a sieve. Sprinkle the remaining redcurrants over the fruit, pour over the mango purée, garnish with strawberry leaves and chill for at least 1 hour before serving.

29

30

Dress cooked diced beetroot with 120 ml/4 fl oz dry sherry, 1 tsp sugar, 1 tbsp wine vinegar, salt and pepper and chill for 30 minutes.

Another wonderful Mexican dish is Chilli con Carne. Soften 2 chopped onions in 3 tbsp oil then add 1 crushed clove garlic, 2 tsp each ground cumin and paprika and 1 chopped green chilli. Cook for 1 minute. Add 450 g/1 lb mince and allow to brown then stir in 400 g/14 oz canned tomatoes, 3 tbsp tomato purée, 1 tsp dried oregano, 1 bay leaf and 120 ml/4 fl oz beer. Cover and simmer for 1 hour, stirring occasionally. Stir in 100 g/4 oz each drained canned red and white kidney beans, pinto beans and chick peas and cook for a further 15 minutes.

Mexican Seviche

450 g/1 lb cod fillets
juice and grated rind of 2
    limes
1 shallot, chopped
1 green chilli pepper, seeded
    and chopped
1 tsp ground coriander
1 green pepper, sliced

1 red pepper, sliced
1 tbsp chopped fresh parsley
1 tbsp chopped fresh
    coriander
4 spring onions, chopped
2 tbsp olive oil
salt and pepper
1 small lettuce, shredded

Don't be put off by the thought of eating raw fish as the cod will 'cook' in the spicy marinade and the result is absolutely delicious.

Skin the cod and cut it into thin strips across the grain. Place them in a bowl and pour over the lime juice. Add the lime rind, shallot, chilli and ground coriander and stir well. Cover and refrigerate for 24 hours, stirring occasionally.

When ready to serve, drain the fish and stir in the peppers, herbs, spring onions and oil. Season to taste and serve on a bed of lettuce.

Serve the salad with a bowl of crispy tortilla chips which give a wonderful contrast in flavour and texture.

July

*'I sing of brooks, of blossoms, birds, and bowers:
Of April, May, of June, and July-flowers.'*
Robert Herrick

Hɪɢʜ summer – the month
for the soft and melting, richly coloured, ripest summer
fruits. Enjoy the warmth of the air, blue skies and
scudding clouds. Unearth the barbecue and picnic basket
and eat outdoors when you can, for you'll have to take
your chances as they come. Save the warmth of the
kitchen for cloudy and showery days when you can make
jams, fools and pies from the strawberries and
raspberries you picked on brighter days.

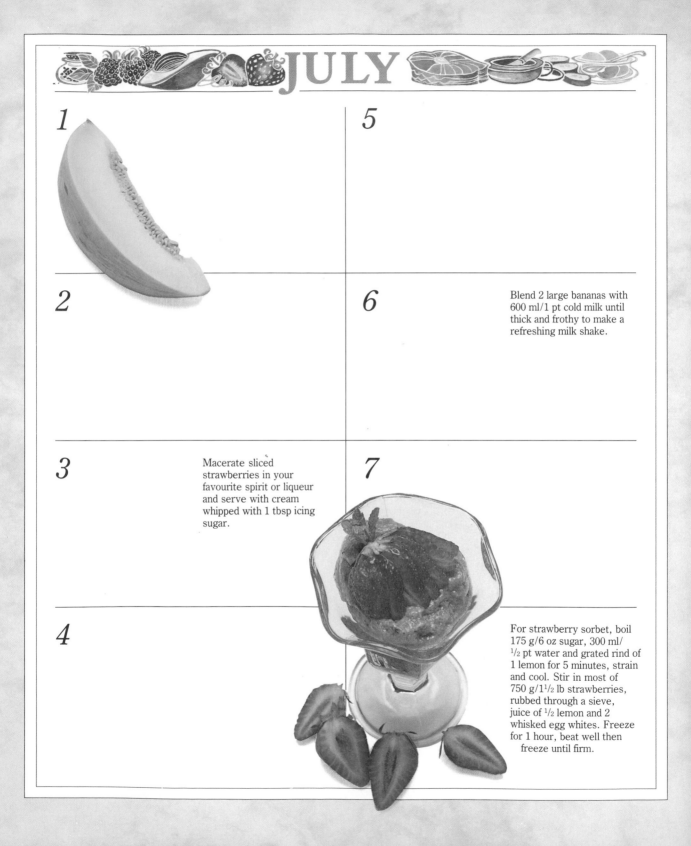

JULY

1

2

3 Macerate sliced strawberries in your favourite spirit or liqueur and serve with cream whipped with 1 tbsp icing sugar.

4

5

6 Blend 2 large bananas with 600 ml/1 pt cold milk until thick and frothy to make a refreshing milk shake.

7 For strawberry sorbet, boil 175 g/6 oz sugar, 300 ml/ 1/2 pt water and grated rind of 1 lemon for 5 minutes, strain and cool. Stir in most of 750 g/11/2 lb strawberries, rubbed through a sieve, juice of 1/2 lemon and 2 whisked egg whites. Freeze for 1 hour, beat well then freeze until firm.

Strawberry Frost

450 g/1 lb strawberries, hulled
1 large banana
175 ml/6 fl oz fromage frais

a few drops of vanilla essence
1 tsp clear honey

Put half the strawberries in the refrigerator. Halve or quarter the remaining strawberries, chop the banana coarsely and freeze them together until solid. Just before serving, place the frozen strawberries and bananas in a food processor with the fromage frais, vanilla essence and honey and process until smooth, pushing the mixture down 2 or 3 times. Divide between individual serving dishes and garnish with the reserved strawberries. Serve at once.

You can buy strawberries almost all the year round now, but they are at their best in midsummer when they are ripe, red and juicy with plenty of flavour. For a change, the recipe also tastes delicious made with raspberries.

8

Throw a few herb sprigs on the barbecue coals when you are grilling to give simple foods added flavour.

12

9

13

Noisettes of lamb are perfect for the barbecue. They can be marinated in oil and herbs or just sprinkled with herbs, brushed with oil and grilled.

10

14

11

To make Spiced Tomato Juice, simmer 750 ml/ 1 1/4 pts tomato juice, 150 ml/1/4 pt water, 1 tbsp sugar, 1 tbsp lemon juice, 1 tsp Worcester sauce, 1 tsp ground cloves, 1/2 tsp cayenne pepper and a pinch of salt for 20 minutes. Strain and chill.

Lamb Kebabs

750 g/1½ lb lean lamb,
cubed
juice of 1 lemon
6 tbsp olive oil
1 clove garlic, crushed

1 tbsp chopped fresh oregano
1 tbsp chopped fresh thyme
salt and pepper
12 fresh bay leaves
2 onions, sliced into rings

Place the meat in a bowl. Mix together the lemon, oil, garlic, herbs and seasoning, pour over the meat and stir well. Cover and marinate in a cool place for at least 4 hours.

Thread the meat on to skewers, alternating with bay leaves. Slip the onion rings over the meat. Grill under a preheated grill for about 10 minutes, turning frequently and basting with the marinade. Serve with rice, salad or grilled peppers.

You can add other vegetables to the kebabs if you wish. Chunks of pepper, mushrooms, onion wedges or courgette slices all taste delicious with lamb. To avoid wooden skewers charring while cooking, soak them in water before preparing the kebabs.

Make kebabs with kidneys, fish, chicken, turkey, pork or beef. Choose ingredients which take about the same time to cook.

15 St Swithin's Day

16 Make Summer Cocktail with Campari poured over crushed ice in a tall glass and topped with fresh orange juice.

17

18

19 For the best flavour, buy free-range or corn-fed chicken rather than battery chickens, which can be very bland.

20

21 To stone an avocado, cut the fruit in half lengthways and twist the two halves apart then lift the stone out of the centre. Always prepare avocado at the last minute and toss in or brush with lemon juice, otherwise the fruit will turn brown.

Chicken and Avocado Salad

8 anchovy fillets
6 tbsp milk
1 spring onion, chopped
2 tbsp chopped fresh tarragon
3 tbsp snipped fresh chives
4 tbsp chopped fresh parsley
300 ml/^{1}/$_2$ pt mayonnaise
2 tbsp tarragon vinegar

150 ml/^{1}/$_4$ pt natural yoghurt
a pinch of sugar
a pinch of cayenne pepper
1 head lettuce, shredded
450 g/1 lb cooked chicken,
   diced
1 avocado
1 tbsp lemon juice

Soak the anchovy fillets in milk for 30 minutes then drain, rinse and pat dry. Purée all the ingredients except the lettuce, chicken, avocado and lemon juice in a food processor. Refrigerate for at least 1 hour.

Arrange the lettuce in the base of a serving bowl, top with the chicken and spoon over the dressing. Peel, stone and cube the avocado and toss immediately in the lemon juice to prevent discolouration. Sprinkle over the salad and serve immediately.

This dressing can be served with a tossed green salad or as a dip for vegetable crudités. Cut fresh carrots, cucumber and multi-coloured peppers into julienne strips and cauliflower into tiny florets and arrange attractively around a pot of the dip.

JULY

22

23
Fold puréed summer fruits into whipped cream and serve with crunchy biscuits for a simple summer dessert.

24

25

26
Sliced tomatoes are delicious layered with a sprinkling of sugar. Pour on French dressing and chill for 1 hour.

27

28
A more unusual Spanish cold soup can be made by pounding 75 g/3 oz almonds and 1 clove garlic to a fine paste with a little water. Beat in 75 g/3 oz fresh breadcrumbs, 6 tbsp olive oil, 1 tbsp sherry vinegar and about 600 ml/1 pt water. Season to taste and serve chilled.

As a garnish for the soup, chop 1 onion, ½ cucumber, 3 skinned tomatoes and ½ green pepper. Arrange some of the garnish on top of the soup and offer the rest separately. Or you can use croûtons, chopped spring onions or red onions, red or yellow peppers.

Originally, gazpacho was pounded in a mortar and pestle in vast quantities to feed hungry farm workers returning from the fields.

Gazpacho

1 green pepper, chopped
8 tomatoes, skinned, seeded and chopped
1 large cucumber, peeled and chopped
1 large onion, chopped
150 g/5 oz French bread, crusts removed

750 ml/1¼ pts water
salt and pepper
2 cloves garlic, crushed
3 tbsp olive oil
2 tbsp tomato purée (optional)
3 tbsp red wine vinegar

Mix together thoroughly all the vegetables and the bread, breaking it into small pieces by hand. Add the wine vinegar, water, salt, pepper and garlic. Purée the mixture, in batches if necessary, until smooth. Beat in the oil and tomato purée, if using. Cover and chill for at least 2 hours.

Whisk again thoroughly before serving.

29

31

Curries do not have to be very hot. A mild chicken curry made with banana, pineapple or coconut make a good summer meal.

30

Try an Indian Carrot and Grape Salad. Cut 3 carrots into julienne strips and mix with 225 g/8 oz seedless grapes. Mix 2 tbsp oil, 1 tbsp honey, 1 tbsp white wine vinegar, 2 tsp lemon juice, 1 tsp crushed mustard seeds and a pinch of pepper. Toss with the carrots and grapes and sprinkle with paprika.

Chilled Fish Curry

225 g/8 oz salmon fillet
375 g/12 oz white fish fillet
300 ml/¹/₂ pt fish or chicken
   stock
salt and pepper
120 ml/4 fl oz mayonnaise
450 ml/³/₄ pt natural
   yoghurt

2 tsp curry powder
juice and grated rind of
   ¹/₂ lemon
100 g/4 oz cooked peeled
   prawns
1 kiwi fruit, sliced
1 sprig fresh mint
1 tbsp flaked coconut

Place the fish in a shallow pan and just cover with stock.
Season to taste and simmer gently for about 15 minutes
until the fish is just cooked. Remove the fish from the
liquid and leave to cool slightly. Mix together the
mayonnaise, yoghurt, curry powder, lemon juice and rind.
Flake and de-bone the fish and mix it into the sauce with
the prawns. Garnish with kiwi fruit, mint and coconut
flakes and serve with boiled rice or new potatoes and a
crisp mixed salad.

There are many types of
rice available. Brown rice is
the unprocessed grain and
needs more water and
longer cooking.

Long-grain rice grains
will stay separate for
savoury dishes. Risotto
rice is a medium-grain,
arborio or Italian rice. Round
pudding rice goes soft and
mushy when cooked.

August

'Dry August and warme,
Doth harvest no harme.'
Anon

THE HOLIDAY month and
the barbecues continue! Colours change from the reds of
July fruits towards the gold of the first harvests.
International flavours creep into the kitchens from all
corners of the holiday world as new ideas return from
sun-baked beaches. Gather in all these influences and
absorb them into your repertoire to give new slants on
old favourites and sunnier ways to enliven your
summer table.

AUGUST

1

5

2

6

Diced cucumber and melon mixed with prawns, seasoned and dressed with mayonnaise make a lovely summer starter.

3

Purée 350 g/12 oz cooked carrots, 2 cloves garlic, 300 ml/$^1/_2$ pt yoghurt, $^1/_2$ tsp each coriander and paprika as a tasty dip with raw vegetables

7

4

Don't just choose honeydew, look out for different varieties of melon. Gallia and Cantaloupe melons are small, round and sweet with a net-like pattern on the skin. Ogen melons are speckled green and highly succulent. Charentais are paler green with an orange, fragrant flesh.

Melon and Prosciutto

1 large ripe Gallia or
    Honeydew melon
16 thin slices
    prosciutto crudo

4 sprigs fresh flat-leafed
    parsley

Halve the melon, scoop out and discard the seeds and
fibres. Peel away the skin and cut the melon flesh into 16
thin slices. Wrap each piece in a slice of prosciutto and
arrange on a serving dish. Chill well and garnish with
parsley before serving.

You can serve olives, stuffed
eggs and sliced salami with
this recipe if you wish, or
replace the melon with
fresh figs.

What we more often call
Parma ham is really
prosciutto crudo, for not all
prosciutto, in fact, comes
from Parma. The hams
are rubbed with a
mixture of salt, spices,
sugar and mustard
and matured to
produce a fine
quality raw ham.

8

12

Buy tuna marked 'dolphin-friendly', to help stop fishermen killing dolphins and other sea creatures caught in their drift nets.

9

Serve summer green beans cooked in boiling salted water until just tender and tossed with chopped onion fried in olive oil.

13

10

14

11

For an unusual summer drink, purée the flesh of 3 ripe mangoes with ½ tsp ground ginger, ½ tsp ground cinnamon, 300 ml/½ pt orange juice and a dash of lemon juice. Serve in wine glasses decorated with a thin slices of orange.

Salade Niçoise

1 head cos lettuce
1 hard-boiled egg, quartered
1 tomato, quartered
6 anchovy fillets
10 black olives, stoned
1 tbsp capers
1/4 cucumber, diced
1 can tuna fish, drained

4 large artichoke hearts,
    quartered
6 tbsp olive oil
2 tbsp red wine vinegar
1/2 clove garlic, crushed
1 tsp mustard
1 tsp lemon juice
salt and pepper

Wash the lettuce thoroughly and tear into bite-sized pieces.
Toss with the other salad ingredients, taking care not to
break up the eggs. Whisk together the dressing
ingredients and pour over the salad just
before serving.

You can use frozen or canned artichoke hearts, but small tender fresh ones will need to be prepared. Cut off the stem, pull the leaves apart and scoop out the hairy choke. Remove the outer leaves down to the tender heart then drop them in water with 1 tbsp lemon juice.

15

Pour a spoonful of Cointreau over wheels of orange and grapefruit segments and garnish with chopped borage.

19

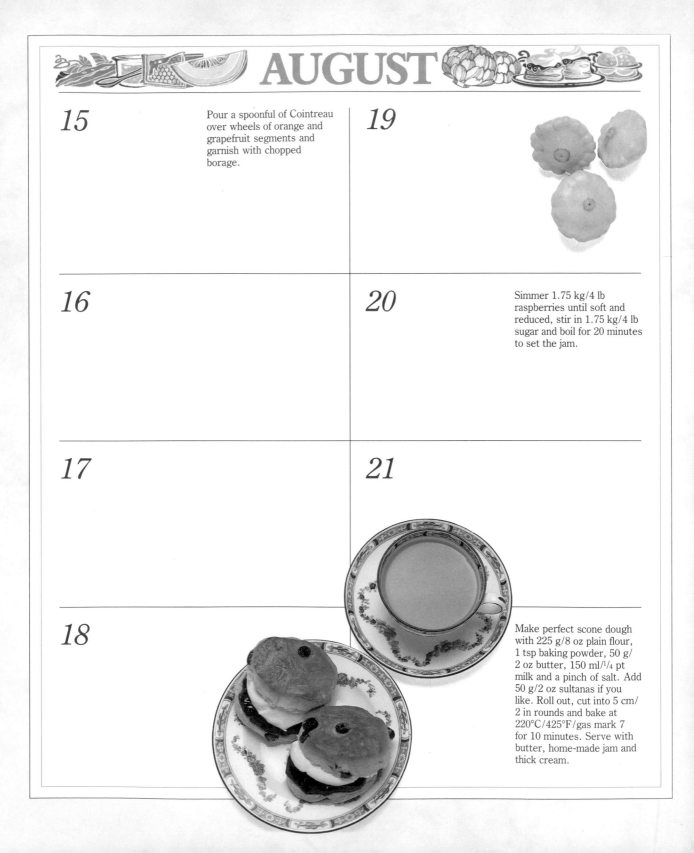

16

20

Simmer 1.75 kg/4 lb raspberries until soft and reduced, stir in 1.75 kg/4 lb sugar and boil for 20 minutes to set the jam.

17

21

18

Make perfect scone dough with 225 g/8 oz plain flour, 1 tsp baking powder, 50 g/ 2 oz butter, 150 ml/¼ pt milk and a pinch of salt. Add 50 g/2 oz sultanas if you like. Roll out, cut into 5 cm/ 2 in rounds and bake at 220°C/425°F/gas mark 7 for 10 minutes. Serve with butter, home-made jam and thick cream.

Honey-Spice Oranges

300 ml/¹/₂ pt clear honey
450 ml/³/₄ pt water
6 sprigs fresh mint

12 cloves
4 large oranges

Bring the honey, water, 2 sprigs of mint and the cloves to the boil in a heavy-based saucepan. Stir until the honey has dissolved, then boil for 5 minutes until syrupy. Leave to cool then strain. Pare the rind very thinly from 1 orange and cut it into very fine shreds. Put the shreds into a bowl, cover with boiling water and leave to stand until cold. Drain well and stir into the syrup. Remove all the skin and pith from the oranges and slice into thin rounds. Arrange on individual plates, pour over the chilled syrup and garnish with the remaining mint.

Honey gives sweetness as well as a delicious flavour to the syrup; try using a particular flower variety for a special taste. The syrup absorbs the flavour of the cloves and mint while boiling. Be sure to remove all the orange pith, otherwise this will give a bitter flavour.

AUGUST

22

23

24

Dissolve 3 tbsp sugar in
5 tbsp water, pour over
4 peeled, cored and halved
pears in a bowl and steam
for 20 minutes.

25

26

27

Boil 225 g/8 oz walnuts for
10 minutes, drain, dry, roll
in 100 g/4 oz sugar and dry
in a cooling oven for 2 hours.
Deep-fry until golden then
cool on a wire rack.

28

Chinese dried mushrooms
add a distinctive flavour and
aroma to Chinese dishes,
and they can be used in this
recipe instead of the pork.
Soak the mushrooms in hot
water for about 30 minutes
until soft then squeeze
out any excess moisture
and remove the tough
stems before slicing
the caps.

Pork and Prawn Chow Mein

225 g/8 oz Chinese noodles
2 tbsp groundnut oil
225 g/8 oz pork fillet, sliced
1 carrot, shredded
1 red pepper, thinly sliced
75 g/3 oz bean sprouts

50 g/2 oz mangetout
1 tbsp rice wine or dry sherry
2 tbsp soy sauce
100 g/4 oz cooked peeled
  prawns

Cook the noodles in boiling salted water for about 5 minutes, rinse under hot water and drain well. Heat the oil in a wok and stir-fry the pork for 5 minutes until almost cooked. Add the carrots and cook for 1 minute. Add the pepper, bean sprouts, mangetout, wine or sherry and soy sauce and cook for 2 minutes. Add the noodles and prawns and toss over the heat for 2 minutes. Serve immediately.

Stir-fry blanched broccoli florets in 1 tbsp oil with a small piece of grated ginger root to serve with this dish.

To make your own bean sprouts, wash 4 tbsp mung beans, cover with cold water and soak overnight. Rinse in cold water, put them into a clean glass jar and secure the top with a piece of muslin. Store in a warm, dark, dry place, rinsing the beans three times a day through the muslin for about 4 days.

29

31

Insert a cocktail stick into a chunk of cucumber. Start to slice it to the centre, turning as you cut, to make a cucumber spiral garnish.

30

For a Sherry Cobbler, put plenty of crushed ice into a tall glass and half-fill with sherry. Add a splash of orange Curaçao and a

teaspoon of fruit syrup and stir. Garnish with a sprig of fresh mint and a slice of orange and lemon.

To make a Summertime Soda, mix together the juice of 1 orange, 1 lemon and 1 grapefruit. Pour over ice cubes, top up with soda water to taste and float a scoop of vanilla ice cream in the top. Serve with straws and a spoon.

For a refreshing Coconut Cooler for party drivers, mix together 1 litre/1³/₄ pts grapefruit juice, 1 litre/ 1³/₄ pts pineapple juice and 225 g/8 oz soft creamed coconut. Chill well before serving.

Tipsy Cake

400 g/14 oz canned fruit
    cocktail
5 tbsp sweet sherry
50 g/2 oz ratafia biscuits
6 trifle sponges, cut into
    wedges
3 tbsp raspberry jam

50 g/2 oz flaked almonds
2 tbsp cornflour
25 g/1 oz vanilla sugar
300 ml/$\frac{1}{2}$ pt milk
1 egg, beaten
300 ml/$\frac{1}{2}$ pt whipped cream
3 glacé cherries, halved

Drain the fruit. Mix a quarter of the juice with 4 tbsp of sherry. Reserve a few of the ratafias for decoration and crumble the remainder. Slice the sponges in half, spread with the jam and cut each one diagonally. Arrange one-third of them in the bottom of a glass bowl. Cover with half the fruit, sprinkle with half the biscuits and almonds and pour over one-third of the juice and sherry mixture. Repeat this, then top with the remaining sponges and juice.

Mix the cornflour and sugar with a little milk. Bring the rest of the milk almost to the boil, stir it into the cornflour mixture then return it to the pan. Bring to the boil, stirring, and simmer for 1 minute. Stir in the remaining sherry and egg then cool until lukewarm. Pour over the trifle, allowing some to trickle down into the bowl. Chill then decorate with whipped cream, glacé cherries and the reserved ratafias.

This is a good way of using up stale sponge cake, or you can use sponge fingers. Sliced ginger cake layered with thinly sliced pears, seasoned with nutmeg and topped with custard also makes a delicious trifle.

September

'The rule is, jam to-morrow and jam yesterday –
but never jam today.'
Lewis Carroll

GOLD turns to purple as
the late fruits ripen on the trees and hedgerows. This is
the month for plums and damsons, for enjoying the last of
the late summer evenings and picking your own
blackberries from the tangled hedgerows. Steam up the
lengthening evenings making jams and chutneys ready for
the winter store cupboard. Pick up on old traditions:
prepare pickled onions for your Christmas table and think
about baking your Christmas cake to give it time to
mature. Enjoy the traditional home-grown varieties of
apples and pears while you still can.

SEPTEMBER

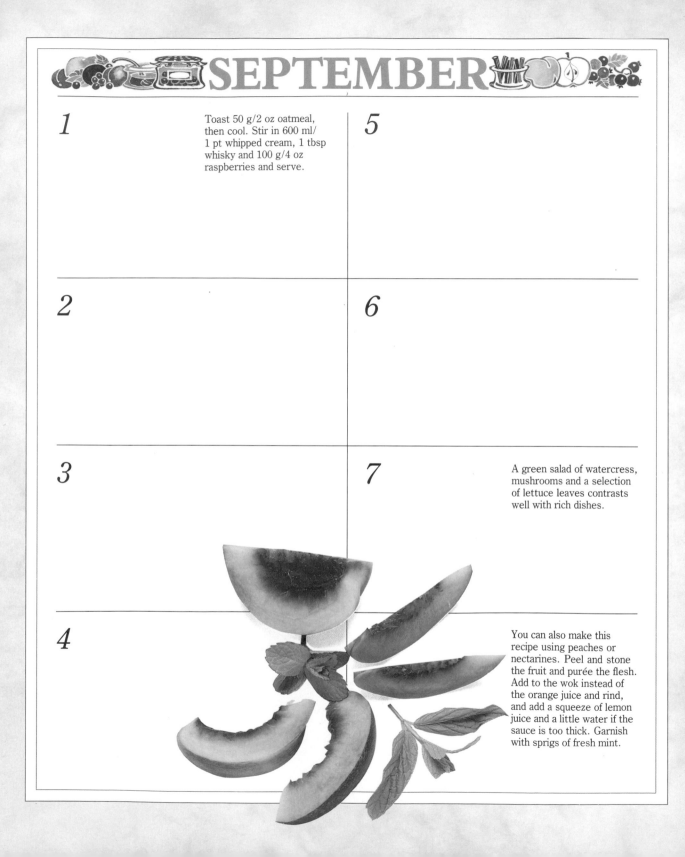

1 Toast 50 g/2 oz oatmeal, then cool. Stir in 600 ml/ 1 pt whipped cream, 1 tbsp whisky and 100 g/4 oz raspberries and serve.

2

3

4

5

6

7 A green salad of watercress, mushrooms and a selection of lettuce leaves contrasts well with rich dishes.

You can also make this recipe using peaches or nectarines. Peel and stone the fruit and purée the flesh. Add to the wok instead of the orange juice and rind, and add a squeeze of lemon juice and a little water if the sauce is too thick. Garnish with sprigs of fresh mint.

Duck with Orange

3 oranges
1 duck
15 g/¹/₂ oz butter
1 tbsp oil
300 ml/¹/₂ pt chicken stock
6 tbsp dry red wine
2 tbsp redcurrant jelly
salt and pepper
1 tsp arrowroot
1 tbsp water
1 sprig watercress

Pare the rind thinly off 2 of the oranges and cut into fine shreds. Put the rind in a bowl, cover with boiling water and leave until cool, then drain. Squeeze the juice from 2 oranges. Cut away the peel and pith from the remaining orange and slice into thin rounds. Wash and dry the duck.

Heat the butter and oil in a wok and brown the duck all over. Remove the duck from the wok, cool slightly and cut away the leg and wing ends. Cut the duck in half lengthways then cut each half into 1.5 cm/1 in strips. Remove the fat from the wok and return the duck to the wok. Add the stock, wine, redcurrant jelly, strips of orange rind and orange juice, bring to the boil and season to taste. Cover and simmer gently for 20 minutes or until well cooked. Skim any fat from the surface. Mix the arrowroot and water and stir it into the sauce. Bring back to the boil and simmer for 5 minutes until the sauce is thick. Arrange on a warmed serving plate and garnish with the orange slices and watercress. Serve with roast or duchesse potatoes and green beans.

Use a sharp knife or poultry shears to cut the duck into 2.5 cm/1 in strips.

SEPTEMBER

8

12

Deep-fried sprats make an excellent starter with brown bread and butter. Fry in batches and serve very hot.

9

Boil 100 g/4 oz sugar and 150 ml/¹/₄ pt water then poach grapefruit slices for 6 minutes. Add 4 tbsp brandy and serve hot or cold.

13

10

14

11

Serve squid rings with a selection of dips. Make your own mayonnaise or use a good brand. To individual pots of mayonnaise, add: 1 clove garlic, crushed; 1 tsp curry powder; chopped mixed herbs; ¹/₂ chopped onion, 1 tsp Worcester sauce and 50 g/2 oz crumbled blue cheese.

Crispy Squid Rings

750 g/1¹/₂ lb squid
50 g/2 oz plain flour
salt and pepper

oil for deep-frying
1 lemon, cut into wedges
2 sprigs fresh parsley

Lemon offers a sharp taste contrast to fried foods, especially with fresh parsley or oregano. A mixture of prawns, shelled scallops and squid rings taste good cooked in this way. Do not overcook them, though, or they will go rubbery.

Hold the body of the squid and pull away the tentacles and head. Remove and discard the intestines and plastic-like quill. Cut off the head and beak and remove the skin. Separate the tentacles and cut the body into rings. Mix the flour, salt and pepper and toss the squid in the flour. Heat the oil and fry the squid in batches for about 3 minutes until golden brown and crisp. Drain on kitchen paper and sprinkle with salt. Arrange on a warmed serving dish and garnish with lemon wedges and parsley.

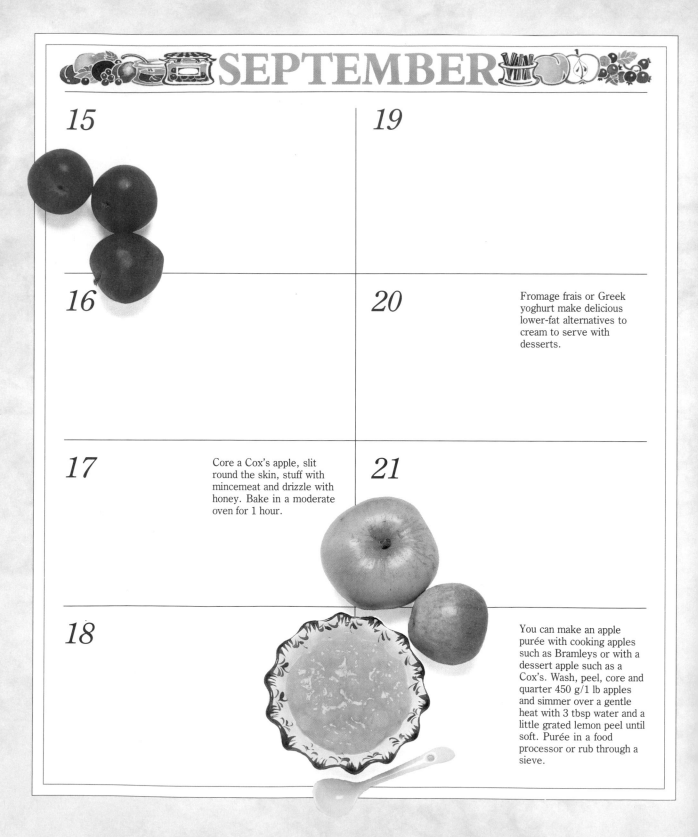

SEPTEMBER

15

16

17

Core a Cox's apple, slit round the skin, stuff with mincemeat and drizzle with honey. Bake in a moderate oven for 1 hour.

18

19

20

Fromage frais or Greek yoghurt make delicious lower-fat alternatives to cream to serve with desserts.

21

You can make an apple purée with cooking apples such as Bramleys or with a dessert apple such as a Cox's. Wash, peel, core and quarter 450 g/1 lb apples and simmer over a gentle heat with 3 tbsp water and a little grated lemon peel until soft. Purée in a food processor or rub through a sieve.

Apple and Honey Tart

75 g/3 oz butter
75 g/3 oz wholewheat flour
75 g/3 oz plain flour
3 egg yolks
3 tbsp water

300 ml/¹/₂ pt apple purée
4 tbsp honey
2 tbsp ground almonds
2 eating apples, thinly sliced

Rub the butter into the flours. Beat 1 egg yolk with 2 tbsp
of water and mix into the flours to form a soft dough,
adding more water if necessary. Roll out and line a
greased 23 cm/9 in flan ring. Prick the base with a fork
and flute the edges. Mix the apple purée with 1 tbsp of
honey, the remaining egg yolks and the ground almonds.
Spread over the pastry and arrange the apple slices on top.
Bake in a preheated oven at 190°C/375°F/gas mark 5
for 40 minutes. Warm the remaining
honey and brush over the
warm tart.

Brushing the tart with the
honey while it is still warm
gives it a wonderful rich
glaze. You can use a honey
glaze on any similar tarts, or
on fruit cakes or
tea breads.

SEPTEMBER

22

Sliced red cabbage steamed with sliced apples is a good accompaniment for rich dishes such as beef or goose.

26

23

27

24

Choose a tasty but light starter – such as deep-fried mushrooms in breadcrumbs or fresh tomato soup – before a strongly flavoured meal.

28

25

To make Sauerkraut and Potatoes, boil 450 g/1 lb sliced potatoes until just tender; do not drain. Fry 2 sliced onions and 100 g/4 oz chopped bacon in 2 tbsp oil and add to the potatoes with 450 g/1 lb sauerkraut. Season and thicken with 1 tbsp cornflour. Simmer for 30 minutes until thick.

German Pepper Steak

4 x 100 g/4 oz sirloin or
  rump steaks
2 cloves garlic, crushed
salt and pepper
2 tbsp oil
2 shallots, finely chopped
4 tbsp capers
100 g/4 oz mushrooms,
  sliced
2 tbsp plain flour
300 ml/¹/₂ pt beef stock
1 tbsp French mustard
2 tsp Worcester sauce

120 ml/4 fl oz dry white
  wine
2 tsp lemon juice
a pinch of dried thyme
a pinch of dried rosemary
8 baby ears of corn
1 green pepper, sliced
1 red pepper, sliced
2 chilli peppers, seeded and
  halved
4 ripe tomatoes, skinned
  and sliced

This is an unusual and tasty recipe which goes well with boiled rice or sauté potatoes. You can substituted canned pimento for the fresh red peppers if you prefer, and sliced dill cucumbers can be added with the tomatoes.

Germans often drink beer with meals rather than wine, so try serving this with a glass of chilled German lager.

Rub the steaks on both sides with garlic, salt and pepper. Heat half the oil in a frying pan and seal the steaks on both sides then remove them from the pan. Add the remaining oil and fry the shallot, capers and mushrooms for 1 minute. Stir in the flour and cook for 1 minute. Stir in the stock, mustard, Worcester sauce, wine, lemon juice and herbs and bring to the boil. Add the corn and peppers and return the steaks to the pan. Cook for about 5 minutes until cooked to your liking then transfer the steaks to a warmed serving plate. Add the chillies and tomatoes to the pan, reheat and spoon the sauce over the steaks to serve.

SEPTEMBER

29 Michaelmas

30

Simmer peeled chestnuts in chicken stock for 30 minutes until tender. Remove the chestnuts, season the sauce with salt and cayenne and boil to reduce by half before pouring over the chestnuts.

September is the month for damsons and plums so make your jams and pickles now.

For Damson Chutney, put 1.5 kg/3 lb stoned damsons, 450 g/1 lb cored and minced apples, 3 chopped onions, 450 g/1 lb sultanas, 900 g/2 lb mixed preserving and brown sugar, 1.2 litres/2 pts vinegar, 2 tbsp salt, 2 tsp ground ginger, 2 tsp ground cinnamon and 1 tsp allspice in a preserving pan. Boil for about 3 hours until thick, stirring frequently. Pour into warmed jars, seal and label. Store in a cool, dry place ready for Christmas.

To make Damson Jam, place 2.75 kg/6 lb stoned damsons in a preserving pan with 600 ml/1 pt water. Bring to the boil and simmer until pulpy. Stir in 2.75 kg/6 lb warmed sugar and boil rapidly for about 5 minutes to setting point.

To test for setting, put a spoonful of jam on a cold saucer. If the jam wrinkles when pressed, it is ready. If not, boil for 4 minutes and test again.

Devilled Poussins

4 poussins
1 tsp paprika
1 tsp mustard powder
1 tsp ground ginger
1/2 tsp ground turmeric
a pinch of ground allspice
50 g/2 oz butter, melted
2 tbsp chilli sauce
4 springs watercress

1 tbsp plum chutney
1 tbsp brown sauce
1 tbsp Worcester sauce
1 tbsp soy sauce
a dash of tabasco sauce
3 tbsp chicken stock

Tie the legs of each poussin together and tuck them under the wing tips. Mix together the 5 spices, rub them all over the poussins and refrigerate for at least 1 hour. Arrange the poussins in a roasting pan and brush with the butter. Roast in a preheated oven at 180°C/350°F/gas mark 4 for 20 minutes, basting occasionally. Mix together all the remaining ingredients except the watercress and brush half the mixture over the poussins. Cook for a further 40 minutes, brushing with the remaining sauce so that the skins become brown and crisp. Serve garnished with watercress.

Pasta shells go well with this dish. To cook pasta, bring a saucepan of salted water with 1 tbsp oil to the boil, add the pasta and stir. Return to the boil and boil until just tender but still slightly firm - *al dente*. Drain well and toss with butter.

October

*'How well I know what I mean to do
When the long, dark autumn-evenings come.'*
Robert Browning

As THE leaves turn and the
days grow shorter and colder, the colours of autumn
pervade the scene: russet and orange, yellow and gold.
Even the colours in the kitchen reflect the autumn glow of
firelight as pheasant and partridge come into season to be
roasted to crispness, and russet apples still make those
favourite puddings and crumbles. The autumn is at its
height when the sun shines on a golden October day.

1

5

Make garlic croûtons to serve with soup by frying cubes of bread in olive oil with 2 crushed cloves of garlic.

2

If you have to keep mussels overnight, wrap them in damp newspaper and keep in the tray at the bottom of the refrigerator.

6

3

7

4

Either Dublin Bay or Mediterranean prawns can be used instead of large prawns for a spectacular flavour and visual effect. Dublin Bay prawns are really a small lobster and are served in restaurants as scampi. Both are available all the year round, fresh or frozen, and are usually sold cooked.

Provençale Fish

1 onion, chopped
2 cloves garlic, crushed
3 tbsp olive oil
750 g/1½ lb tomatoes,
    skinned and chopped
600 ml/1 pt dry red wine
2 tbsp tomato purée

salt and pepper
900 g/2 lb mussels, scrubbed
    and bearded
8 large prawns
100 g/4 oz peeled prawns
4 crab claws, shelled

Fry the onion and garlic gently in the oil for 5 minutes until soft but not brown. Add the tomatoes and fry until just soft. Stir in the wine and tomato purée, season and bring to the boil. Cover and simmer for 15 minutes. Add the mussels, cover and simmer for 5 minutes until all the mussels have opened. Discard any that do not open. Stir in the remaining ingredients and cook, uncovered, for 8 minutes until heated through.

You can buy crab claws fresh or frozen. Crack the shell very carefully with a hammer or nutcrackers and remove the flesh in one piece, retaining the shape of the claws.

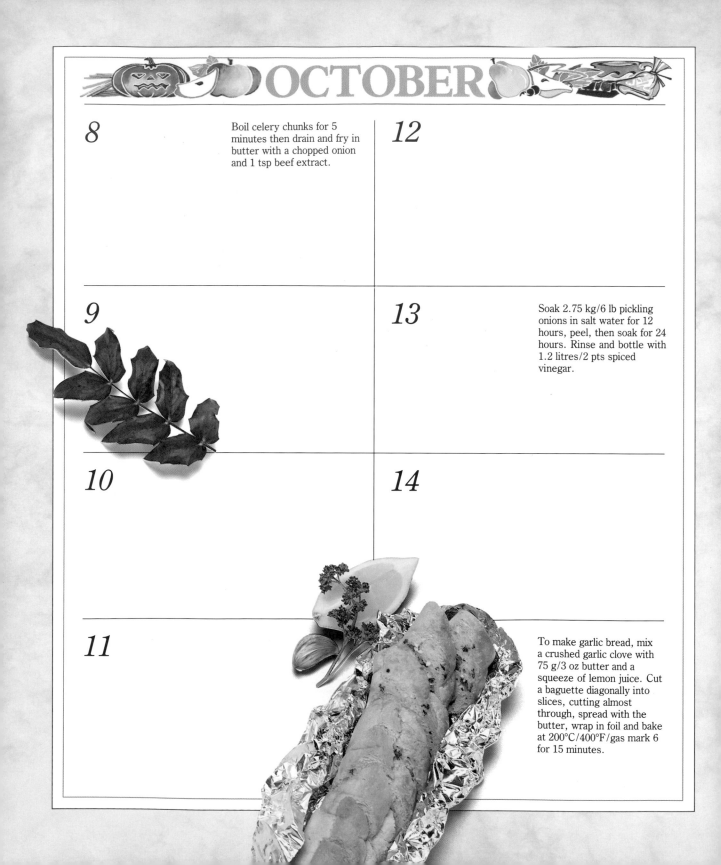

OCTOBER

8

Boil celery chunks for 5 minutes then drain and fry in butter with a chopped onion and 1 tsp beef extract.

12

9

13

Soak 2.75 kg/6 lb pickling onions in salt water for 12 hours, peel, then soak for 24 hours. Rinse and bottle with 1.2 litres/2 pts spiced vinegar.

10

14

11

To make garlic bread, mix a crushed garlic clove with 75 g/3 oz butter and a squeeze of lemon juice. Cut a baguette diagonally into slices, cutting almost through, spread with the butter, wrap in foil and bake at 200°C/400°F/gas mark 6 for 15 minutes.

Baked Spaghetti

225 g/8 oz wholewheat
    spaghetti, cooked
800 g/1³/₄ lb canned
    tomatoes, chopped
1 onion, chopped
1 tsp dried oregano

salt and pepper
100 g/4 oz Cheddar cheese,
    grated
25 g/1 oz Parmesan cheese,
    grated

Grease 4 individual ovenproof dishes and divide the
spaghetti between them. Spoon over the tomatoes, onion
and oregano and season well with salt and pepper. Sprinkle
with the Cheddar and Parmesan and bake in a preheated
oven at 180°C/350°F/gas mark 4 for 30 minutes.

Any kind of long or ribbon
pasta is suitable for this dish
- spaghetti, tagliatelli,
vermicelli or bucatini are the
favourites - fresh or dried,
white, green or wholewheat.

Cook the pasta in boiling
salted water with a dash of
olive oil to prevent the
pieces sticking together.

OCTOBER

15

16

Peel apples as thinly as possible. It is easiest to core them with a round corer, but you can use a sharp knife.

17

18

19

20

Bake puff pastry triangles and lightly fry apple slices in butter. Slice the cooled pastry and sandwich with the apples and fromage frais.

21

For a special dessert, peel 4 pears and scoop out the cores from the base. Stuff with 15 g/½ oz each chopped walnuts and glacé cherries. Melt 100 g/4 oz chocolate, 2 tbsp black coffee, 25 g/1 oz butter and 1 tbsp rum. Beat in 2 eggs yolks then 2 whisked egg whites. Spoon over the pears and chill.

Apples in Overcoats

225 g/8 oz plain flour
a pinch of salt
a pinch of ground cinnamon
a pinch of freshly grated
    nutmeg
100 g/4 oz butter
4 tbsp iced water

4 dessert apples
4 stoned prunes, chopped
4 dried apricots, chopped
1 tbsp raisins
1 egg, beaten
6 sprigs fresh mint
300 ml/¹/₂ pt cream

Mix the flour, salt and spices. Rub in the butter then mix
in enough water to make a smooth dough. Divide into 4
and roll out into 20 cm/8 in squares. Peel the apples and
carefully remove the cores with an apple corer. Mix
together the prunes, apricots and raisins. Place one apple
in the centre of each pastry square and fill the centres with
the fruit mixture. Brush the edges of each square with
water and drawn them up and around the sides of the
apples, sealing them with water and trimming excess
pastry to give a neat finish. Roll out the pastry trimmings,
cut into decorative leaves and stick on to the apples. Brush
with egg and bake in a preheated oven at
180°C/350°F/gas mark 4 for 25 minutes
until golden brown. Garnish with
mint and serve hot with cream.

Use this pastry for any
sweet dishes. For extra rich
pastry, use 1 egg yolk and
reduce the amount
of water.

Cox's apples are particularly
good for this dish as they
have a natural sweetness
and cook well. Firm pears
can also be used for this
recipe and you can stuff
them with any mixture of
dried fruits.

OCTOBER

22

Serve winter dishes with a strong red wine such as Rioja, roast potatoes and a selection of fresh winter vegetables.

26

23

27

Purée 225 g/8 oz cooked chick peas with 1 chopped fried onion, some parsley and 1 egg. Make into patties and fry until golden.

24

28

25

Pheasant are in season from October to January and you can buy them ready-dressed for cooking. Oven-ready frozen pheasants are available all the year round. A hen pheasant is usually considered the tastiest and will serve three to four people; a cock pheasant is slightly larger.

Pheasant in Red Wine

1 tbsp oil
1 tbsp butter
1 large pheasant
2 eating apples, halved and
    cored
1 onion, chopped
1 tbsp plain flour
150 ml/¹/₄ pt stock or water

150 ml/¹/₄ pt dry red wine
finely pared and juice of
    1 orange
2 tsp brown sugar
salt and pepper
1 bay leaf
1 sprig fresh parsley
1 sprig fresh thyme

Heat the oil and butter and brown the pheasant all over then transfer it to a casserole dish with the apples. Fry the onion in the pan until soft then stir in the flour and cook for 1 minute. Stir in the stock or water and wine, bring to the boil, stirring, then add the orange rind, juice and sugar. Season with salt and pepper and pour the sauce over the pheasant. Tie the herbs together with cook's string, add to the casserole, cover and bake in a preheated oven at 180°C/350°F/ gas mark 4 for 1 hour until tender.

Bouquet garni is made with a selection of fresh herbs of your choice, and using the freshest herbs will give the casserole a wonderful flavour. If you do not have fresh herbs, use a sachet of bouquet garni. Remember to remove the bouquet garni before serving.

29

30

Shake together a dash of orange bitters, 1 tbsp each fresh orange juice, red vermouth, white vermouth, Gran Marnier and dry gin for a Halloween Cocktail.

31 Halloween

You can use your pumpkin shell as a halloween lantern as well as an unusual soup bowl. Prepare the shell as described in the recipe, then draw some eyes and a mouth on one side. Cut them out carefully with a sharp knife. Cut a hole in the lid and tie some string to each side of the shell to make a handle. Sit a night light in the base of the lantern and replace the lid.

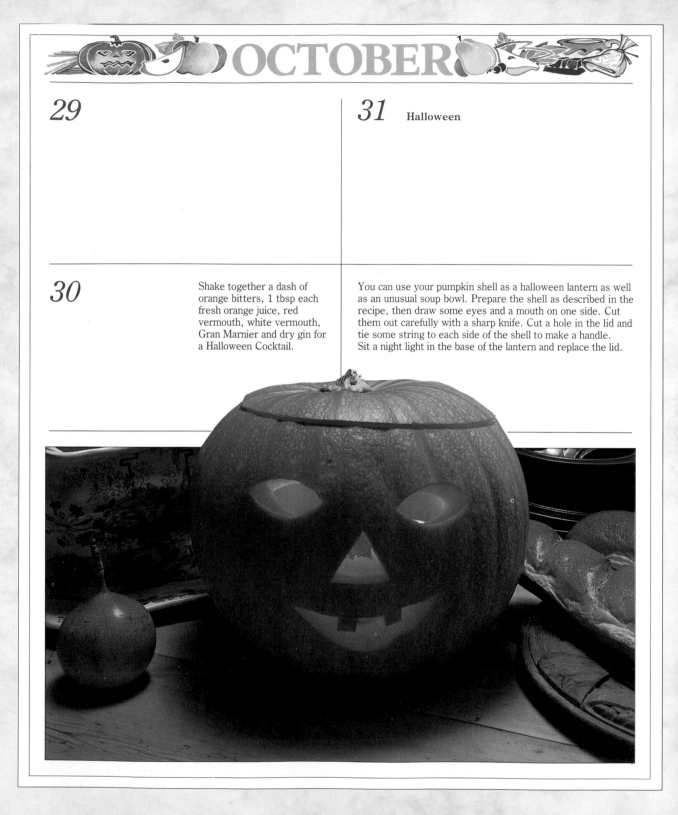

Pumpkin Soup

1 x 1.5 kg/3 lb pumpkin
4 tbsp butter
1 large onion, sliced
1 litre/1³/₄ pts water
250 ml/8 fl oz double cream

a pinch of freshly grated
*   nutmeg*
salt and white pepper
1 tbsp snipped fresh chives

Wash the pumpkin well and cut around the outside of the stem about 5 cm/2 in away from it. Carefully cut most of the pulp off the top and reserve the lid. Remove and discard the seeds. Use a spoon to scoop out all but 1 cm/½ in of pulp from inside without piercing the outer skin. Chop the pumpkin pulp. Melt the butter and fry the onion gently for 5 minutes until soft but not brown. Add the pumpkin and water, bring to the boil, cover and simmer gently for 20 minutes. Purée, return to the pan and add the cream, nutmeg and seasoning.
Reheat and pour into the pumpkin shell. Garnish with snipped chives.

Use a metal spoon to scoop out and discard the stringy pulp and seeds. Carefully remove the pulp with a spoon or small knife to make a shell.

November

'No shade, no shine, no butterflies, no bees,
No fruits, no flowers, no leaves, no birds, –
November!'
Thomas Hood

THOUGH the skies can
be cold and grey and the landscape takes on the bleak,
empty of look of winter after the raging beauty of
autumn, the warmth of the kitchen can offer winter
delights to banish the cold. Nothing warms like a rich
soup of fresh root vegetables, sweetened with carrots
and parsnips and thickened with barley. Nothing is more
cheering than a steaming suet pudding bulging with dates
and dripping with syrup. And there's bonfire delights,
too, to keep us busy and set us on the road towards the
real festivities at the end of the year.

NOVEMBER

1

2

3 Whisk hot milky chocolate in a blender until really frothy and serve in a tall mug sprinkled with grated chocolate.

4

5 Guy Fawkes' Night

6 Scrub some large potatoes and prick the skins with a fork. Wrap them in foil and bake them in the embers of the bonfire.

7

Parkin is a traditional bonfire night cake. Blend 100 g/4 oz each self-raising flour, oatmeal, brown sugar and black treacle with 50 g/2 oz butter, 1 egg, 5 tbsp milk and 2 tsp ground ginger. Level in a greased baking tin and bake in a preheated oven at 180°C/350°F/gas mark 4 for 45 minutes.

Spicy Baked Beans

*450 g/1 lb dried haricot
   beans*
100 g/4 oz belly pork
1 onion

1 tsp mustard powder
6 tbsp black treacle
salt and pepper

Soak the beans overnight in water. Drain, transfer to a saucepan and cover with fresh water. Bring to the boil and boil for 10 minutes. Drain and reserve the water. Place the beans, pork and onion in a large deep casserole dish. Mix together the mustard, treacle, salt and pepper with 300 ml/^{1}/$_2$ pt of the bean water and stir into the beans. Add enough bean liquid to cover the ingredients, exposing only the rind of the pork. Cover the casserole and bake in a preheated oven at 150°C/300°F/gas mark 2 for 2 hours. Stir in the remaining liquid and cook for a further 1^1/$_2$ hours until the beans are tender, uncovering for the last 30 minutes. Remove and discard the onion. Remove the pork, cut off and discard the rind, dice the meat and return it to the dish. Adjust the seasoning and serve with sausages.

Dissolve 175 g/6 oz brown sugar, 15 g/^{1}/$_2$ oz butter, 50 g/2 oz syrup, 5 tbsp water, ^{1}/$_2$ tsp vinegar then boil to 143°C/290°F when a drop snaps in cold water. Stick wooden skewers into 6 apples, dip in toffee then in cold water and stand them on a greased tray. Wrap well if not to be eaten quickly.

NOVEMBER

8

9
Serve pancakes with
different bacons: dry cured,
smoked and green rashers,
or fry bacon bits until crisp
and brown.

10

11

12
Twist some rinded streaky
bacon rashers in a spiral
round a skewer. Grill until
crisp then remove the
skewer to serve.

13

14
Serve Mulled Cider hot in
mugs. Bring 1.2 litres/2 pts
dry cider to the boil with
4 tbsp muscovado sugar and
a pinch of salt. Tie 4 cloves,
a 5 cm/2 in piece of cinnamon
stick, 4 allspice berries and a
strip of orange peel in muslin
and add to the pan. Cover
and simmer for 15 minutes.

Boxty Pancakes

225 g/8 oz potatoes, grated
225 g/8 oz mashed potatoes
225 g/8 oz plain flour
1 tsp salt
1 tsp bicarbonate of soda
50 g/2 oz butter, melted
4 tbsp milk
salt and pepper
2 tbsp oil

Mix the potatoes and mashed potatoes. Mix together the flour, salt and bicarbonate of soda and stir them into the potatoes. Stir in the melted butter and just enough milk to make the mixture into a batter of dropping consistency. Season with salt and pepper. Heat the oil in a griddle or heavy-based frying pan and fry spoonfuls of the batter until crispy and golden on both sides.

You can make similar potato pancakes with 450 g/1 lb grated raw potatoes, 2 chopped onions, 50 g/2 oz chopped bacon, 1 egg, 50 g/2 oz plain flour. Mix together to a batter with a little milk if necessary and fry gently until cooked through and golden brown.

NOVEMBER

15

Simmer 225 g/ 8 oz soaked split peas until tender, drain and mix with 1 chopped, fried onion, 1 egg, salt and pepper. Bake at 180°C/ 350°F/gas mark 4 for 30 minutes.

19

16

20

17

Only cook mangetout or green beans until just tender to maintain their flavour and wonderful crisp texture.

21

18

Serve ham with sweet potatoes and okra. Boil scrubbed sweet potatoes in salted water for 25 minutes. Boil okra for 15 minutes, or fry 1 chopped onion and 1 clove garlic in oil, add the okra and fry for 5 minutes. Add 3 tbsp water, $^1/_2$ tsp turmeric, salt and pepper, cover and simmer for 15 minutes.

Use a small sharp knife to remove the rind from the ham, leaving the fat as smooth as possible. Score quite deeply into diamond shapes and stud with cloves for extra flavour and to give an attractive appearance.

You can use 100 g/4 oz honey instead of cola or you can boil the ham for the first half of the cooking time.

Cola Glazed Ham

4.5 kg/10 lb joint smoked gammon
1.2 litres/2 pts cola

225 g/8 oz dark brown sugar
cloves

Soak the ham overnight. Place rind side down in a roasting pan, pour over all but 3 tbsp of the cola and bake in a preheated oven at 180°C/350°F/gas mark 4 for 2½ hours, basting frequently. Remove the ham from the oven and leave to cool for 15 minutes. Remove the rind and score the fat to a depth of 5 mm/¼ in. Stick a clove in the centre of every other diamond. Mix together the sugar and the remaining cola and spoon over the ham. Raise the oven temperature to 190°C/375°/gas mark 5 and bake for a further 25 minutes, basting frequently. Cover loosely with foil if the ham begins to brown too much. Allow to stand for 15 minutes before slicing.

NOVEMBER

22

23

24

Root vegetables such as carrots, beetroots and parsnips were all common ingredients in 18th century cakes and puddings.

25

26

27

Fry 3 sliced courgettes and 1 bunch sliced spring onions in 1 tbsp each sunflower and sesame oil and sprinkle with sesame seeds.

28

Carrot flowers make a colourful garnish. Peel a carrot then cut into 5 cm/ 2 in lengths. Cut v-shapes lengthways down the carrot and remove the strips. Cut the carrot into thin slices. Arrange to resemble flowers, using caviar or a clove for the centres, chive stems and cucumber skin leaves.

Courgette and Carrot Layer

1 onion, chopped
450 g/1 lb courgettes,
    chopped
1 tbsp oil
100 g/4 oz ground almonds
75 g/3 oz wholemeal
    breadcrumbs
1 tsp vegetable concentrate
1 egg, beaten

1 tsp dried mixed herbs
1 tbsp tomato purée
1 tbsp soy sauce
pepper
450 g/1 lb cooked, mashed
    carrots
1 sprig fresh rosemary
2 sprigs fresh parsley
1 carrot, cut into strips

Fry the onion and courgettes in the oil for 5 minutes until soft. Add the remaining ingredients except the carrots, rosemary and parsley and mix together well. Place half the courgette mixture in a greased and lined 450 g/1 lb loaf tin and press down well. Arrange the mashed carrots on top and cover with the remaining courgette mixture.
Cover with foil and bake in a preheated oven at 180°C/350°F/gas mark 4 for 1 hour.
Allow to cool for 10 minutes before removing from the tin and garnishing with rosemary, parsley and carrot.

Rosemary is a highly aromatic herb which goes well with both vegetable and meat dishes, although it should be used in moderation. It is a perennial herb which originates from the Mediterranean but grows well in British gardens.

29

30

Get ahead for Christmas by making Spiced Cranberry Preserve with the cranberries appearing in the shops. Place 450 g/1 lb cranberries and 300 ml/¹/₂ pt cider vinegar in a pan with a 1 cm/ ¹/₂ in piece of cinnamon stick, a 1 cm/¹/₂ in slice root ginger and 1 tsp whole allspice tied in muslin. Bring to the boil and simmer for 25 minutes until the cranberries are soft and the skins pop. Stir in 225 g/8 oz demerara sugar and simmer for 20 minutes. Remove the spices and pot in warmed jars.

Carrots are plentiful now, so try a tasty Carrot Cake. Cream 225 g/8 oz each butter and brown sugar. Beat in 4 egg yolks, grated rind of ¹/₂ orange and 3 tsp lemon juice. Stir in 175 g/6 oz self-raising flour, 1 tsp baking powder, 50 g/2 oz ground almonds, 100 g/4 oz chopped walnuts and 350 g/12 oz grated carrots. Fold in 4 whisked egg whites and spoon into a greased and lined 20 cm/8 in cake tin. Bake in a preheated oven at 180°C/350°F/ gas mark 4 for 1¹/₂ hours. Beat together 225 g/8 oz cream cheese with 2 tsp clear honey and 1 tsp lemon juice, spread over the cooled cake and sprinkle with chopped walnuts.

Almond Lattice

175 g/6 oz frozen puff pastry
100 g/4 oz butter
100 g/4 oz caster sugar
2 eggs
1 tsp baking powder
1/2 tsp almond essence

1 tbsp milk
100 g/4 oz plain flour
4 tbsp damson jam
50 g/2 oz almond paste,
    grated

Use two-thirds of the pastry to line a greased 25 cm/10 in flan tin allowing 2.5 cm/1 in overlap all round. Roll out the remaining pastry and cut into 1 cm/1/2 in strips. Cream the butter and sugar. Beat in the eggs one at a time then the almond essence and milk, adding a little flour between each addition. Fold in the remaining flour. Spread the jam over the pastry case and sprinkle with the almond paste. Cover with the sponge mixture. Make a lattice with the pastry strips, dampen and crimp the edges, turning in the overlap of pastry to form a rim. Bake in a preheated oven at 200°C/400°F/ gas mark 6 for 20 minutes then at 180°C/350°F/gas mark 4 for a further 15 minutes.

This makes a large tart, but you can reduce the quantities or make two smaller tarts and freeze one. Almonds impart a distinctive flavour to this recipe. If you like a crunchier topping, sprinkle with flaked almonds before putting on the pastry lattice.

December

'At Christmas play and make good cheer,
For Christmas comes but once a year.'
Thomas Tusser

WHO NEEDS reminding to
enjoy the festive season? For December builds up to that
wonderful climax when all the preparations, the work and
the planning come to fulfilment. And so much of that
enjoyment revolves around the kitchen, where succulent
turkey and goose, crisp Brussels sprouts, sweet
parsnips, crunchy and melting potatoes, rich puddings
and tipsy sauces are prepared, decorated and brought
steaming to the table.

DECEMBER

1

2

Fresh parsley will keep well
if stored in a glass of water
or in a sealed container at
the bottom of the
refrigerator.

3

4

5

For a tasty alternative,
winter stews can be topped
with rounds of scone dough
(Aug 15) for the final 20
minutes of cooking.

6

7

To make Irish Soda Bread,
mix 225 g/8 oz plain flour,
450 g/1 lb wholewheat flour,
2 tsp each cream of tartar
and bicarbonate of soda,
1 tsp each salt and sugar,
450 ml/³/₄ pt milk and 1 tbsp
yoghurt. Knead into a round
and cut a cross on top. Bake
at 200°C/400°F/gas mark 6
for 40 minutes.

This is an ideal recipe for making use of your slow cooker, especially if you are out at work all day.

Irish Stew

900 g/2 lb boned mutton or lamb
900 g/2 lb potatoes, sliced
3 onions, sliced
salt and pepper
2 tbsp chopped fresh parsley
1 tsp chopped fresh thyme
375 ml/13 fl oz water

Trim the meat, leaving on a little of the fat. Season the meat and vegetables with salt, pepper, 2 tsp of parsley and the thyme. Layer the potatoes, meat and onions in a large casserole, starting and finishing with a layer of potatoes. Add the water and cover tightly. Cook in a preheated oven at 140°C/275°F/gas mark 1 for 2½ hours, shaking occasionally to prevent sticking. Check now and again that the liquid has not dried out. The potatoes will thicken the finished stew so it should not be too runny. Brown the top under a hot grill and sprinkle with the remaining parsley.

Slice the potatoes quite thinly for this dish. You will get the best results if you use a mandolin slicer or a food processor but a sharp knife will be fine if you make sure you slice thinly.

DECEMBER

8

For Sweet White Sauce, cook 50 g/2 oz butter and 2 tsp cornflour for 1 minute, whisk in 1 tsp sugar, 300 ml/½ pt milk and cook for 3 minutes.

12

9

13

Brussels sprouts are excellent at this time of year. Serve them tossed in butter and sprinkled with toasted flaked almonds.

10

14

11

Brandy or Rum Butter are a must with Christmas pudding. Cream 100 g/4 oz butter until soft then beat in 75 g/3 oz sugar and the grated rind of ½ orange and 3 tbsp brandy or rum. Chill in small bowls and serve with the pudding, or pop a knob under the lid of warmed mince pies.

Christmas Pudding

100 g/4 oz wholewheat
   self-raising flour
225 g/8 oz shredded suet
225 g/8 oz raisins
100 g/4 oz sultanas
100 g/4 oz mixed peel

25 g/1 oz chopped almonds
grated rind of 1 lemon
$1/2$ tsp freshly grated nutmeg
2 eggs, beaten
2 tbsp clear honey
150 ml/$1/4$ pt milk

Mix together the flour, suet, fruit, peel, almonds, lemon rind and nutmeg. Whisk together the eggs and honey and mix into the dry ingredients with the milk. Spoon into a greased pudding basin, cover with pleated greaseproof paper and a pudding cloth and secure with string. Place the pudding in a saucepan with about 4 cm/1½ in water, cover and steam for 3 hours, topping up with boiling water as necessary. Cool and re-cover with clean greaseproof and cloth and store in a cool, dry place. When ready to eat, steam for 1½ hours.

Made with vegetarian suet, this is perfect for all your Christmas guests, served with a glass of sweet dessert wine.

DECEMBER

15

16

17

Make festive garnishes for biscuits or cakes with coloured almond paste cut into holly or ivy leaves, Christmas trees, Santas or robins.

18

19

As a contrast to rich traditional dishes, serve simply grilled mackerel with mashed potatoes.

20

21

Make vegetable bundles as an attractive garnish. Trim carrots, courgettes, cucumbers, peppers or celery into 3 mm/¹/₈ in matchsticks about 5 cm/2 in long. Soften strips of green spring onion in boiling water and use them to tie up the bundles.

Spiced Beef

2.75 kg/6 lb brisket of beef
3 bay leaves, finely chopped
1 tsp ground mace
1 tsp ground cloves
1 tsp crushed black
   peppercorns

1 large clove garlic, crushed
1 tsp salt
1 tsp ground allspice
2 tbsp molasses
3 tbsp brown sugar
450 g/1 lb cooking salt

It takes time for the meat to absorb the spices and flavourings which tenderise the joint whilst imparting their wonderful tastes.

Place the beef in a large dish. Mix together all the spices and flavourings and rub well into the meat. Cover and refrigerate for 24 hours. Repeat this process every day for a week, turning the meat and rubbing in the spices which will be mixed with the juices drawn from the meat. Tie the meat up firmly in a round and place in a saucepan. Cover with water and simmer gently for 6 hours. Leave in the cooking liquid until cool enough to handle then place in a dish and cover with a weighted plate. Slice very thinly to serve.

Served cold and thinly sliced, this is a great Christmas dish. It takes a little time, but is not difficult to prepare.

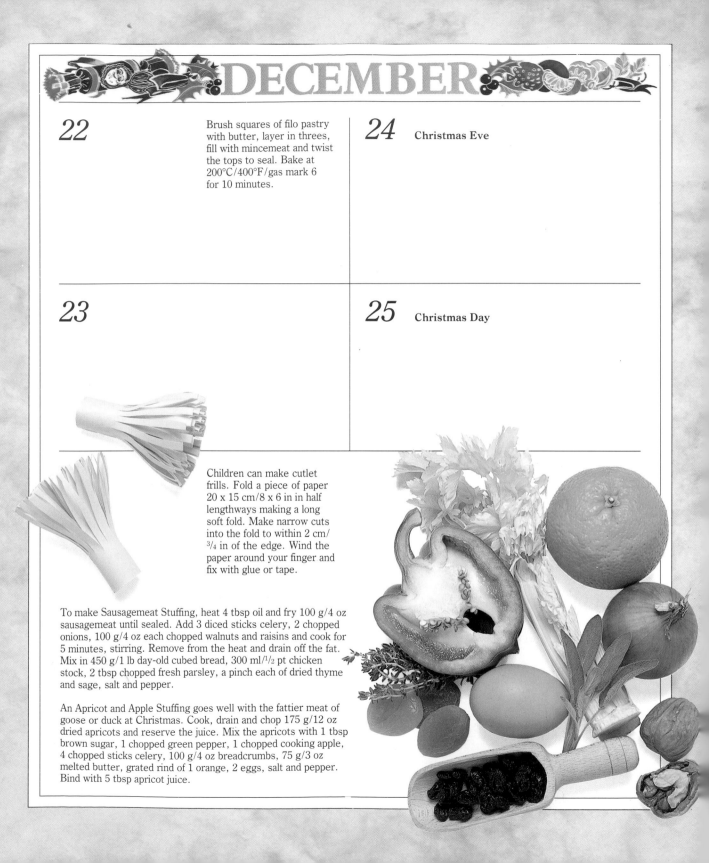

22

Brush squares of filo pastry with butter, layer in threes, fill with mincemeat and twist the tops to seal. Bake at 200°C/400°F/gas mark 6 for 10 minutes.

24

Christmas Eve

23

25

Christmas Day

Children can make cutlet frills. Fold a piece of paper 20 x 15 cm/8 x 6 in in half lengthways making a long soft fold. Make narrow cuts into the fold to within 2 cm/$^3/_4$ in of the edge. Wind the paper around your finger and fix with glue or tape.

To make Sausagemeat Stuffing, heat 4 tbsp oil and fry 100 g/4 oz sausagemeat until sealed. Add 3 diced sticks celery, 2 chopped onions, 100 g/4 oz each chopped walnuts and raisins and cook for 5 minutes, stirring. Remove from the heat and drain off the fat. Mix in 450 g/1 lb day-old cubed bread, 300 ml/$^1/_2$ pt chicken stock, 2 tbsp chopped fresh parsley, a pinch each of dried thyme and sage, salt and pepper.

An Apricot and Apple Stuffing goes well with the fattier meat of goose or duck at Christmas. Cook, drain and chop 175 g/12 oz dried apricots and reserve the juice. Mix the apricots with 1 tbsp brown sugar, 1 chopped green pepper, 1 chopped cooking apple, 4 chopped sticks celery, 100 g/4 oz breadcrumbs, 75 g/3 oz melted butter, grated rind of 1 orange, 2 eggs, salt and pepper. Bind with 5 tbsp apricot juice.

Christmas Turkey

1 x 7 kg/16 lb turkey   *6 tbsp butter*

Use tweezers to remove any feathers on the bird. Remove the fat just inside the cavity. Stuff the neck cavity of the bird with the sausage stuffing, packing in as much as possible. Place the remaining stuffing in an oiled casserole dish and cover. Tie the turkey legs together without crossing them over. Tuck the neck skin under the wing tips and sew up with string. Place the turkey on a rack in a roasting pan and spread some of the butter over the breast and legs. Cover loosely with foil and bake in a preheated oven at 160°C/325°F/gas mark 3 for 2½ hours, basting frequently. Remove the foil and continue to roast for a further 2 to 2½ hours until the juices run clear when the thickest part of the thigh is pierced with a skewer. Cook the stuffing for the last 45 minutes of the cooking time. Cover the turkey and leave to stand for 20 minutes before carving.

DECEMBER

26   Boxing Day

30

27   Fry slices of leftover Christmas pudding in butter, dust with sugar and serve with 150 ml/^{1}/$_4$ pt double cream whipped with 1 tbsp icing sugar and 2 tbsp port.

31   New Year's Eve

28

To make Champagne Cocktail, drop a lump of sugar into a Champagne flute and soak it with Angostura bitters. Add a couple of dashes of brandy and top with chilled Champagne. Garnish with a slice of orange and a cherry.

29

Spiced Nut Cake

225 g/8 oz plain flour
1 tsp baking powder
225 g/8 oz caster sugar
a pinch of salt
a pinch of freshly grated
   nutmeg
a pinch of ground ginger
120 ml/4 fl oz orange juice

2 tbsp butter, melted
4 tbsp water
1 egg, beaten
100 g/4 oz cranberries
100 g/4 oz hazelnuts,
   chopped
1 tbsp icing sugar

You can replace the hazelnuts with chopped walnuts or almonds, and use multi-coloured glacé cherries and mixed peel instead of the cranberries.

Sift together the dry ingredients and make a hole in the centre. Stir in the orange juice, butter, water and egg. Beat together until all the flour is incorporated. Stir in the cranberries and nuts. Grease and line a 22 x 12.5 cm/ 9 x 5 in loaf tin. Spoon in the mixture and bake in a preheated oven at 160°C/325°F/gas mark 3 for 1 hour until a skewer inserted into the centre comes out clean. Remove from the tin, peel off the paper and dust with icing sugar. Slice and serve warm or cold with butter or cream cheese.

Index of Recipes

Dates refer to the first date on each spread.